It has been said that to perpetuate the myth tha Robertson beg to differ. The worst kind of passive inves into buying expensive and investor (self-directed, low-cost and diversified index fund shareholders) is a Pilgrim's Progress for all of us. Read their fast-paced story--- and it is a story, not a lecture--- and you'll learn all the basics for mastering the investing side of personal finance. Steve and Dan are living proof that active saving and simple investing can produce millionaires.

—Scott Burns, Personal Financial Columnist,
Universal Press Syndicate

Pure, unadulterated and honest financial advice from a couple guys who have persevered through everything life has thrown at them. It's rare to get such a personal account of someone's financial life, Late Bloomer Millionaires is really a financial memoir. Steve and Dan walk you through their financial lives and give you an all access pass to their struggles, triumphs, defeats and their victories. I can tell you this, you will NOT read another personal finance book like this one. It is more than just a financial book, it's a heartwarming journey of love, relationship and growth that uses personal finance as the central theme. This is nonfiction at its best and an adventure worth experiencing. By the end you will feel smarter and empowered financially and full of hope that you can do this thing called life...I mean, retirement!

—Scott Dauenhauer CFP, MSFP, AIF
[scott@meridianwealth.com]

I met Steve and Dan more than a decade ago when they were fighting to get better retirement investment options for teachers. Late Bloomer Millionaires explains how they learned the often hard-knock investing lessons that got them there and provides the wisdom of experience that can help you.

—Kathy Kristof, author of Investing 101

Steve and Dan discuss their failures and triumphs in this lovely narrative on how they navigated the muddy waters that are retirement planning and came out on top. Their story helps demystify the do-it-yourself approach to retirement planning and proves that anyone can do it, even those later in their careers. A fantastic and informative read for anyone looking to thrive in retirement, not just survive.

—Crystal Mendez, 5th Grade Teacher,
Los Angeles Unified School District (LAUSD)

Steve Schullo and Dan Robertson have written a very personal account of their quest for financial security for their retirement in their book, Late Bloomer Millionaires. Their journey takes them from investing in TSAs to the high flying tech stocks to index funds. Even when they lost about two-thirds of their portfolio in the tech crash, Dan and Steve did not give up. They eventually found a sound way to invest their funds. This book gives good information to any investor who is unsure about what to do with their retirement funds. The authors are role models for anyone who is still unsure about what to do to ensure their own secure retirement.

— Joe MacDonald, retired LAUSD elementary teacher

I enjoyed it immensely. As an author, I know the work Steve and Dan put into their valuable creation. It reflects a beautiful life together!

—Taylor Larimore, Bogleheads' Investment Forum founder and co-author of two books, The Bogleheads' Guide to Investing and the Bogleheads' Guide to Retirement Planning

In Late Bloomer Millionaires, authors Steve Schullo and Dan Robertson relate their life's investing experiences, openly admitting to doing lots of things wrong, then showing how they made midstream corrections as they learned more and more about investing. After a number of false starts, and some gut-wrenching losses in the tech-wreck, they eventually righted their investing ship and found their path to financial independence. The lessons they learned and the advice they give in the book can help keep readers from making the same mistakes. Their experience shows that it's never too late to get on the right path to financial success. Read it and reap!

—Mel Lindauer, Forbes.com columnist and co-author, The Bogleheads' Guide to Investing and The Bogleheads' Guide to Retirement Planning

Steve Schullo and Dan Robertson fill a real void with Late Bloomer Millionaires. Hopefully, the title doesn't deter young Americans as well as mid-career professionals from taking its sage advice. The strategies they share for creating and managing investment portfolios, selecting financial advisors and even increasing personal savings are helpful guides to retirement security for those of any age.

—Carolyn Widener, Community College trustee, California State Teachers Retirement System (CalSTRS), 2001-2011

Steve and Dan aren't Wall Street insiders. They are real people, with a real financial story, that real people can learn A LOT from. Really!

—Dan Otter, author of 3 financial books, teacher, webmaster of 403bwise.com and crusader for 403b reform

Reading Late Blooming Millionaires, I felt I was right there alongside the authors on the road to financial freedom. In its pages is an indictment of today's withering 403b options for public educators, who surely deserve more than what current tax law and the California insurance code calls for.

—Brad Rumble, Elementary Principal, LAUSD

If you're worried about your retirement, intimidated by the complexity of investing, or have had bad experiences with Wall Street firms and commissioned based advisors, Steve Schullo and Dan Robertson have written the book for you. They show you that you don't have to make the same mistakes they made. Instead you can learn from their experiences. The best part is that Steve and Dan show you that the winning strategy is actually quite simple, something Wall Street doesn't want you to know. Appendix C which covers 65 key points showing you the difference between the loser's game Wall Street wants you to play- short-term thinking/sales pitches—and the winners game of long-term thinking/objective information, is worth the price of the book by itself.

—Larry Swedroe, Principal and Director of Research, The Buckingham Family of Financial Services

If you've saved and lost or never saved at all, this is the book for you. It's never too late is the financial theme of "Late Bloomer Millionaires." Steve Schullo and Dan Robertson lost their hard-earned retirement funds due to bad investment advice from greedy advisors and the authors' mistakes. That's when they took matters into their own hands and through painstaking research and self-education managed to recoup their losses as well as a wealth of knowledge. Now they are self-made millionaires and they tell you in captivating detail how they did it. No boring economic geek-speak here. Instead they relay their easy-to-understand strategies through personal stories and anecdotes. So whether you're saving for retirement or are already retired, "Late Bloomer Millionaires" is a must-read.

—Karen Westerberg Reyes Retired Special Projects Editor of AARP The Magazine

"What makes this book different from most other financial books on the market today is the willingness of Steve and Dan to share their mistakes, as well as their successes. Their candid experience demonstrates how reactions to mistakes can reshape our future.

As tireless advocates of low cost investing for their fellow teachers, they have chosen to share their message with a wider audience, and for that, we can be thankful. For those of you who may have thought that you have waited too long to practice sound financial values, you will be glad to know that it is never too late to start applying the ideals Steve and Dan outline here."

—Eric Goldberg, Certified Financial Planner (CFP)

Steve and Dan take us on an amazing candid financial journey, where they leave the baggage of high expenses and emotions back at the station and venture out on a new path toward diversification and discipline. Reading this book offers the reader an outstanding opportunity to learn and profit from both their mistakes and successes.

—Allan Roth - Author, "How a Second Grader Beat Wall Street"

This honest account of a couple's financial journey – learning investment strategies, negotiating the markets, creating wealth (losing it and regaining it back in time for an early retirement)—will be empowering to anyone interested in getting their financial house in order and most of all creating their own wealth. The main message of this book: It is never too late!

—Debora Vrana, former Los Angeles Times financial reporter

What sets this book apart is the riveting personal stories of the authors. In addition, the extended section on selecting and working with an adviser who will put your interests first should prove invaluable to those who recognize the general wisdom of a diversified, low-cost approach to investing, but are not ready to do it totally on their own.

—Alex Frakt, co-founder bogleheads.org

Steve and Dan give the reader insight into their personal lives as well as their investment partnership. Steve relays how difficult it is for a K-12 educator to find a low cost 403b product where any vendor may sell an annuity product. As a colleague of Steve's in the quest for educators to be prepared for retirement, this book gives sound information to all that a secure retirement is possible. Steve and Dan's descriptions of how they were able to reach their goals will be a helpful roadmap to readers.

—Dr. Sandy Keaton, Educational Audiologist, advocate for 403b reform and education; Teachers' Union representative on the district's Retirement Investment Advisory Committee; Chair of the Teachers' Union Pre-Retirement Issues Committee; Chair of the Teachers' Union Investment Workshops and Pre-Retirement Conferences

Steve Schullo and Dan Robertson

Late Bloomer Millionaires

A Financial Story
and Investment Guide
for Late Starters

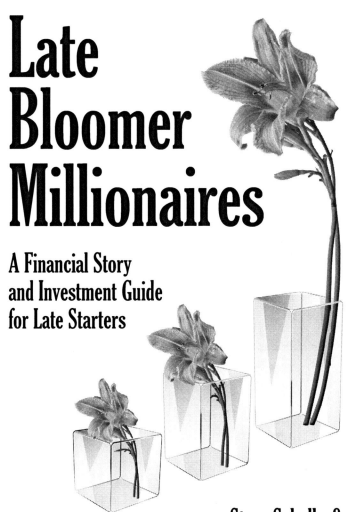

Steve Schullo &
Dan Robertson

Schullo, Steve
Roberston, Dan
Late Bloomer Millionaires

1st edition
LCCN: 2012912722

Published by Late Bloomer Wealth Press
Rancho Mirage, CA
www.latebloomerwealth.com

ISBN: 978-0-9858357-0-5

Editor: John Carrigan, CarriganCommunications.com
Editor: Jeff Wuorio
Cover/interior design: Mark E. Anderson, Aquazebra.com

AQUA EBRA

This book is manufactured in the USA.

Exercise caution in your business affairs,
for the world is full of trickery.
But let this not blind you to what virtue there is;
many persons strive for high ideals,
and everywhere life is full of heroism.

—Part of the Desiderata

There is a choice you have to make,
in everything you do.
So keep in the mind that in the end,
the choice you make, makes you.

—Anonymous

Introduction

"I would never recommend mutual funds; they are too risky for teachers!" Steve's financial adviser's response about retirement investing terminated the discussion. Dan's adviser tells him, "I don't work with mutual funds." These sales pitches backfired—we never talked to these advisers again.

These folks wanted to sell us expensive commissioned-laden annuities. We had to ask: Why do most of us trust others with our money? Don't we know that behind the free pizza or the pastry-to-die-for are flattering sycophants pushing guaranteed, 'no-risk, leave-it-to-me' insurance products and commission-laden mutual funds which skim our gains right off the top? Our solution was simple: armed with scant knowledge about personal finance we realized that the stark remarks revealed conflicts of interest designed to scare us into plans that were never sound investments.

From these financial wake-up calls we discovered our former advisers' comments reflected something much bigger and deeper, a systemic financial epidemic: people anointed to look after our interests—our employers' and the unions' financial consultants and the army of advisers had opposing interests—their own. The slick presentations and enthusiastic claims from the "suits" were too often lies. We discovered that the policy wonks within these organizations whom we think know more than us, don't. It was that simple.

These revelations compelled us to learn the investing process and find a low-cost strategy for retirement investing. With our late-blooming talents of reflection and study, we could not depend on Wall Street cronies for unbiased help—are you kidding? We had no choice but to go it alone in our forties and fifties.

Armed with blossoming optimism and excess confidence, we made our first million with the tech bubble and lost it. We recouped the million dollars after an intense overhaul in time for early retirement. It is our delight to share our story and financial insights complete with disagreements. You will discover how simple it is to recognize and find objective financial information and investing options for the goal of a stable retirement income.

We loved the learning adventure and the challenge of doing something that we had never planned nor wanted to do. We didn't learn to invest independently at a young age though we have always been frugal.

Heck, we didn't start investing seriously until our forties. We wrote this book to help others who think it's too late. We have good news for you—we chronicle how a couple of regular financial consumers did succeed later in life.

We hope you'll enjoy our story with its emotional highs and lows, with the "big picture" perspective and holistic thinking that led to our investing decisions as a couple. We want you to enjoy the journey as we have—unraveling the maze of confusing and intricate financial obstacles to find a less competitive approach to personal finances that leads to a sleep-easy secure retirement. You don't have to be a "late-bloomer" to benefit. We know this is possible. Why? We have done the hard work for you in this book.

Preface

In part I, we write our individual stories in first person "I." For the remainder of the book, we co-write as "we" and "our." It is "our" story, one voice told by both of us with occasional vignettes such as "Steve said this" or "Dan did that." The book is intended to be part memoir with a specific caveat—it's not about us so much as about you discovering the investing process with our observations, reflections and portfolio showing how and what we learned.

Chapter 4 covers the basics of investing and can be skipped by those who know about the DOW and asset classes. The calculations used throughout the book are uncomplicated: basic math.

Financial advisers can see how a couple of ordinary guys applied stock market basics in a comprehensible way which we hope can be useful to build and support an informed and satisfied clientele.

This case study methodology presents our financial evolution from newbies to successful investors. As professional educators we present what we have found for all employees in private and non-profit enterprises.

Steve Schullo and Dan Robertson

Contents

Part I - Our Story

Chapter One: Steve's Story (Before 1993)

What do an immigrant single mom, Minnesota Mining & Manufacturing (3M) and a dairy farm in northern Wisconsin have in common?

Chapter Two: Dan's Story (Before 1993)

As a gay kid in the '50s Dan identified with people who live on the periphery. This led to a career in Special Education and the determination to be self-sufficient. He learned from his father to bypass the middleman.

Part II - Sprouting Our Portfolio

Chapter Three:
Financial Education Begins (1994-2002)

Learning about no-loads, technology sector mutual funds, the dot.com bubble, hitting the million-dollar threshold and crashing.

Chapter Four: Back to Basics (2003)

Fessing-up to mistakes, what were the fundamentals ignored when we joined the tech bubble mania? How does Wall Street classify the stock and bond markets for the individual investor's benefit?

Moving forward with seasoned experience and the discovery of the indexing strategy. Disagreements about the decades old passive/active investing philosophy debate. Dan's metamorphosis.

An exciting year with retirement, relocating and starting anew. How did we do during the Real Estate bubble and the ensuing second crash?

The portfolio grew and funded our early retirement activities. A three-year look at how a balanced low-cost portfolio works and fluctuates with the market. Rebalancing and distributions.

The data behind our story: insights and concepts gleaned after eighteen years of observation, reflection and analyses of the investing process.

Part III - It's Your Turn

Getting started with a simple plan. Several authors and thinkers who created "lazy portfolios."

Tables and Figures

Chapter 11

Chapter 13

Chapter 14

Appendix D

Part One
Our Story

"The easiest way for your children

to learn about money is for you to

not have any."

—Katharine Whitehorn,
British Journalist

Steve Schullo and Dan Robertson

CHAPTER 1

Steve's Story

— BEFORE 1993 —

I learned about the stock market from my eighth-grade educated mother. She was born in Italy in 1909 and immigrated with her parents to St. Paul, Minnesota. She was raised in a convent after her mother's death graduating eighth grade. Her father remarried and started a new family. Instead of attending high school, Linda became the baby-sitter for her younger half-siblings.

Mom married my father in 1930 when she was 21. She moved to his farm a few miles from a small 19th century sawmill settlement now dubbed Wisconsin's "Island City," Cumberland. My parents were excellent role models for living within their means. They owned and managed a 140-acre dairy farm. Mom was in charge of the paperwork. My father was illiterate and his parents (my grandparents) spoke Italian. They sold milk to the local cheese factory and earned $1.50 a month during the Great Depression of the 1930s. Living on that tiny check and making ends meet by growing their food was a constant challenge. Survival was by what *they did* as an extended family rather than what the Great Depression did to them.

In the 1950s my father's health declined and the dairy herd was wiped out with hoof and mouth disease. It was up to mom to become the bread winner. She hired on as an assembly-line worker at the new Minnesota Mining and Manufacturing (3M) satellite factory built in Cumberland. I learned about stocks and shares from her purchase of 3M stock. This was long before most households owned stocks: a remarkable testament to her foresight.

Mom also purchased U.S. Savings Bonds before dad's death in 1961. I don't know how she did it on her meager wages. She also saved the $38 per month *Social Security for Minors* benefit (I was the minor when dad died). She could have spent it but didn't. She saved it for my college education.

When she first told me she wanted me to go to college, I thought, "What the heck is college?" Later, I thought college was for smart city kids. Despite flunking second grade at the neighborhood one-room country school and a deplorable high school record, University of Wisconsin-River Falls accepted me under academic probation. Room, board and tuition cost a thousand dollars—available because of her foresight.

Steve Schullo and Dan Robertson

After my first year of college I enlisted in the Marine Corps (1967).

The Marine Corps made it easy to save. I withdrew $25 out of my $90 monthly pay to buy bonds. When I was discharged two years later from Camp Pendleton, I had saved $500.

I settled in Los Angeles and lived with my sister Lorraine and her family in Norwalk. With her help I found a job, attended Cerritos Junior College, paid for groceries and saved before going on my own. Recurring dreams of the farm were a constant reminder of home. But returning to Cumberland was not an option. What might have seemed an opportunity of a lifetime and envy of many 22 year-old young men, independence and finishing college were more important than inheriting the 80 year-old family farm.

As a self-effacing and insecure country boy living in Los Angeles, I was easily intimidated and lonely. This foreign environment challenged me to grow up, be responsible and self-reliant. I hadn't learned these critical life skills in the Marine Corps. I knew how to do without and live within my own resources while focusing on healthy, affordable activities such as reading and an active outdoor lifestyle.

I valued and took pride in my debt-free attitude. Despite earning minimum wages at dead-end jobs, I was never broke nor borrowed money. Driving a VW bug for years with no payments and living with roommates reduced living expenses. By controlling housing and transportation costs, I saved a little—a simple discovery which would last the rest of my life.

I was always in school (at least part-time) graduating from Los Angeles City College with an AA degree. It took five long years to adapt to big-city life and be outgoing. I became a follower and student of John Boldt's Krafig Gefüel (German for intensive feeling therapy). He was one of many psychological gurus during those turbulent times who pioneered marathon therapy. His Counseling Center in Westwood, near the UCLA campus, served hundreds of people seeking deeper relationships, peace and balance in their lives. It was a crash-course in life that wasn't taught in school. I 'came out' and identified as gay.

At this Center, I experienced the richness of the diversity of people from all walks of life: young, older, attorneys, engineers, CEOs, working class and a celebrity or two. Educated, talented and intelligent people had an amazing range of personal problems. In spite of earning boatloads of money and driving expensive cars, possessing good looks and charm, these characteristics didn't solve difficulties with spouses, parents, bosses, and lovers. I recall Bob, a 30 year-old talented attorney, brilliant in the courtroom, but couldn't talk to his father and had a troubled relationship with his girlfriend! Rich people suffered too—I was flabbergasted.

I thought rich and educated people with all their money, positive attributes of unlimited confidence and intelligence were immune to personal problems.

Was I wrong! I learned a great lesson which would serve me well for the rest of my life: discovering a holistic perspective on personal, social and financial responsibility. After three years of working hard to find out who I am and what the heck am I here for, my life took a giant leap forward. The best thing I got from this humanistic psychology center was meeting Dan.

I knew Dan was the person. We both valued the "inner life," healthy alternative spiritual enlightenment and positive personal development as championed by the center. We opposed many of the short-term distractions of the materialistic, winner-take-all, competitive world. We knew within a few months we would be together for the rest of our lives.

Dan was finishing his doctoral program at UCLA. He supported and encouraged me to quit my job and return to college full time. My savings coupled with a $70 per month Veteran's Disability check (Vietnam injury) and the G.I. Bill of Rights enabled me to take the plunge.

I was petrified, however. Hob-knobbing with thousands of smart fellow students was a daunting adventure. At 28 I was ready, focused and worked hard. I was on the Dean's List after my first quarter. What a turnaround. Even Dan was surprised. My fear of academic failure didn't materialize and the risks I took moving from the country to the big city began to pay off.

I loved college. In a few years I earned my bachelors

and masters degrees in psychology at California State University—Los Angeles, earning a state license to practice psychotherapy (MFCC). I worked at two drug abuse clinics.

At one of these clinics newly hired employees were herded to a benefits presentation. I saw the results of saving $50 a month (paltry by today's standards, but not in 1982). The hypothetical plan earned 5 percent interest over 30 years. I couldn't believe how much could be saved—$41,856, with an $18,000 cash outlay. The power of compound interest and the effects of long-term thinking presented graphically were clear and dramatic—I got it.

I started teaching in 1984 with the Los Angeles Unified School District (LAUSD). This move to a steady career permitted me to save $200 per month in a Tax Shelter Annuity (TSA), my first commitment to retirement saving at age 37.

Annuities are common retirement products for educators (Pre-Kindergarten through 12th grade). The predominance of insurance agents in the schools with the teacher's union approval gave the impression the insurance companies put the educator's needs first.

The agent came to the house for free to explain her products. Having worked in the private sector I knew there were no free lunches. I lost my curiosity about her compensation when she told me the annuity was earning 12 percent interest. Okay, I accepted the situation as presented.

A few years later (1990) I noticed the 12 percent return changed to 10 percent and then 6 percent. The insurance company was resetting the rate every year. When the interest bottomed out at 3 percent, I wondered what the heck happened.

At the time California was beginning an economic recession. My teacher's salary was cut 10 percent and Dan lost his grant funding. I asked my agent to put me into a fund with no surrender fee. She put me into another company. I continued my contributions assuming I could take the money out if needed without the surrender fee. Dan was off for a year and a half writing new grants to fund his next project.

In the meantime we heard annuities were a terrible investment. I decided to stop my TSA contributions until Dan got another job. We started learning about choices in the stock market—mutual funds. Together we saved enough to become proactive in retirement investing and building a portfolio which grows more than a few percent each year.

My knowledge of stocks with a savings account in my local bank and the TSA was a start. I also knew saving a little now produces great effects later. I thought about expanding my investment skills to identify options for growth: real investments and not insurance products. I had these questions:

- What are those numbers reported in the news every day (Dow Jones Industrial Average, S&P 500)?

- What if I invested in a losing company?
- How does the stock market work?
- What are bonds? Mutual Funds? What is a 403(b), 401(k) or 457(b)?
- How do investors protect themselves in a down stock market?
- Who can you trust? How do these people get paid?
- Can I invest in a mutual fund with my 403(b)?

By 1993 we began to find answers to these questions. We learned about the stock market and investing from Louis Rukeyser, Bob Brinker's Radio Show, *Money Talk* and books. Dan subscribed to many financial magazines and a few newsletters. Our shared interest in learning about investing became a fun hobby. We learned how mutual funds work and that anything was better than an annuity.

I was misled into thinking only TSAs are tax-deferred. The IRS code, 403(b), applies to tax-deferred wages for public workers, similar to 401(k) plans in the private sector. Mutual funds are another choice—a fact Dan and I discovered on our own. Dan was not working at the time—he had time to read about the different kinds of mutual funds and search for low-cost companies.

We liked the built-in diversification of hundreds of stocks in a single mutual fund. Mutual funds made the job of selecting investments easy. We were free to transfer between mutual funds at our discretion without surrender fees. We understood markets fluctuate and so would our accounts. Short-term ups and downs didn't matter. We were long-term investors. At the time, I was 46 and Dan was 52, bona fide late-bloomers.

Dan suggested the Vanguard Wellington fund for my 403(b). This fund seemed right for me and I was eager to invest in the stock market. Wellington performed steadily and was low-cost. The allocation has about one-third in bonds and the rest in stocks. This fund fit my objectives and risk tolerance.

I applied for Vanguard Wellington through the school district benefit office to begin my 403(b) contributions. The district's mailed reply was a diagonally scribbled "not available" over my original application. It was way over their head to offer an explanation: cover letter, a name or phone number. "How strange and rude," I thought. The bureaucracy had spoken, not understanding the cursory dismissal of my request. This rejection hit hard. I went through a lot of time and effort to discover, learn and try to take responsibility for my plan.

If you are standing while you read the next couple of paragraphs, you might want to sit down and take a deep breath. My next step was to find out which 403(b) low cost mutual fund companies were available. My district's response to my simple request was stunning.

It started with a routine phone call to the benefits office to request the list of available no-load companies (A "load" is a commission, an up-front cost to purchase many mutual funds or insurance products). The clerk began to read the list of 150 companies available. 125 were insurance companies I didn't want. I interrupted and asked for no-load mutual fund companies. She said she didn't know which mutual fund companies were no-load. All she could do is read the entire list of the mutual fund companies.

I got an inexplicable feeling this wasn't going to go well, but I pressed on.

I asked how many? She said twenty-five and began reading each name as I tried to write them down. I asked her to spell many of the names. Finally, I asked if I could come to the office and get a copy because this was laborious and time-consuming. She said yes, but their policy was for me to copy the list of companies on *my* paper *from their copy*. According to the official district policy, she said, *"No written 403(b) material is released to employees."*

I felt blindsided—I was *not* prepared to debate the merits of this ludicrous policy, so I acquiesced, sat down and took a deep breath. I wrote each of the 25 mutual fund company names, feeling a lot like Alice falling in the rabbit's hole trying to grasp this bizarre world I found facing me head-on over a *list*. Later, I spent a couple of hours researching which of the 25 mutual funds were no loads. So much for assistance.

Why are these people so protective over *a list?* Also baffling, of the 33,000 LAUSD employees contributing to a 403(b), nobody else seemed to complain about this demeaning treatment. Who would have thought my request would be equivalent to Rome's infamous slave, Spartacus, demanding he be declared a Citizen of Rome and a member of the Senate.

INVESCO was an available no-load mutual fund. I filled out the paperwork and began investing in 1994 and for the next eight years. Thus, Dan and I began a decade long million-dollar misadventure.

Steve Schullo and Dan Robertson

CHAPTER 2

In the Beginning for Dan

(BEFORE 1993)

I totaled my dad's '54 Merc on the Pasadena Freeway in 1959. I was 19. My sore chest persisted—I thought I broke a rib from the accident. I went to the University of Southern California (County) Medical Center in East Los Angeles one evening for an emergency X-ray. This hospital treats hundreds of patients from the poorest sections of Los Angeles. The weakly lit unswept hallway was full of gurneys with assorted skid row people waiting their turn for an x-ray, either unconscious or with painful moaning.

It bothered me that some of these patients might need help fast, but if so, it wasn't going to happen. The pace of service, my overwhelming desperation and the realization of being alone at a critical time gave me a horrific scare, especially as a gay kid. This vivid experience showed me the importance of protecting myself from the possibility of ever being on one of those gurneys. This event renewed my resolve to get an education and find a stable profession.

Dad always had a project on the burner: most often mail order. He didn't like having a middleman so he created many mini-businesses: a diet plan, vitamins, or a "work at home" venture. Always the entrepreneur Dad kept his day job, with his progeny employed in the garage assembling mail order products. I saved enough to come home by myself on the Greyhound from New Hampshire as a teenager, buy a Hi-fi, and most of all, appreciate saving money.

Several years later I began my first serious relationship (1960). Sy was a smart, fun ex-New Yorker twice my age. He taught me more about money management, keeping commitments, and how to live well on his budget. I was an undergrad at California State University—Los Angeles (CSULA) with no income for a while. Sy said not to take any job as a way to contribute to our expenses but rather to wait for a career opportunity. "Just be patient," he said.

This was a different life for me, complementing my formal education as I learned to cook while bouncing ideas with my mentor-lover. When I protested that I wasn't pulling my financial weight he said, "Someday you'll help someone else in the same way. Don't worry. That's how it works." Like any good mentor Sy taught me "grown-up" ways.

I started teaching students with learning disabilities in 1962 at the Associated Clinics at CSULA. This opportunity came about because I waited to start a career position as Sy suggested. I did well in a series of summer school classes and the professor offered me the position. Several years later this experience led to a stipend and enrollment in a doctoral program at UCLA. Too much drink killed our good times in about five years. I began a 12-step program which continues. Sy had a fatal motorcycle accident. We had a great start but the end came too soon.

Alan, my first sponsor, gave me great advice: "Save something every month for emergencies." I had taken a hiatus from saving during my drinking years. After a year I had $300.

My friend Jack broke up with his boyfriend and had a round-trip ticket to London available. He gave me the ticket for free. What an extraordinary opportunity to travel. I was surprised at the time and asked my sponsor's advice. He said, "This is what emergency money is for. Go have a great time." And I did.

Jack and I toured London, the Cotswolds, Amsterdam, and drove down the Autobahn to Switzerland. I crammed a lot into those three weeks thanks to Frommer's famous travel guide and the $300.

This magnificent experience was a direct result of planning ahead. I vowed to continue saving after I got home. The following year I took my mom to the Mattehorn in Switzerland.

I was a grad student at UCLA seeking stability in my life when I met Steve at an encounter retreat in Big

Bear in 1975. Within a few months I started a career position at CSULA, managing a job training program for people with disabilities. I learned to write grant proposals. The budgets, objectives, benchmarks and program operations occupied me for more than 25 years.

I was thirty-three and read anyone can retire early with a plan. I picked a retirement age of 59 ½. I enjoyed the challenges of my new job and the new relationship. Steve went back to school as I learned my new tasks. I was able to help Steve as Sy helped me.

When my first annual raise came up it was natural to consider long-term retirement saving. I hadn't forgotten the gurney lesson learned during my hospital wait 15 years prior.

An annuity salesman, Peter, stopped by my office one day. I liked his pitch. He explained "tax-deferred" investing. Money invested in his product would not be taxed until I took it out when I retired. I put $100 a month into a TSA beginning in May, 1976. When I asked about costs, Peter said, "The company pays me." "Oh, that's nice," I thought. Over the next 10 years I bought several annuity products recommended by Peter. Every so often he had a new product with better opportunities for diversity and gains, backed by guarantees.

Subsequently I learned some of them had front-end loads. Others had special charges when a person gets out of them: a surrender charge, or back end load. In addition they charge annual operating expenses, unnecessary insurance and marketing costs. I realized afterward these expenses were eating into my nest egg.

I found a bond fund on my own. After a few years my statement showed a consistent gain of $70 a month for a $6,000 investment. For the first time, I could see my money working for me. It was a turning point to see interest being added to the pot instead of going out. This fund was a better investment than any of the annuities.

This heightened my attention to the market. Steve and I watched financial programs on television. Rukeyser's PBS show on Friday nights was informative and entertaining. But he did not discuss mutual funds.

Richard Ney's 15 minute financial show on an obscure Los Angeles channel was helpful. He provided the perspective "not all is as it seems" on Wall Street. He showed how the stock market floor managers manipulated the market in a manner beyond normal investors' control. His newsletter predicted which parts of the market were next to go up or down. These parts are called sectors, like technology, financial institutions, or energy. He recommended the Fidelity family of funds as a starting place for sector investing.

I subscribed to mutual fund magazines and learned to use mutual funds in our 403(b) plans (not individual stocks). When I asked Peter about mutual funds he said, "I don't work with them." How can the financial advisor who worked with me for 15 years not have a better answer? I was surprised and realized then I had been led down a product-driven path. From then on, I avoided insurance products. I was excited by the opportunity to shift my assets into aggressive-growth mutual funds untainted by loads and surrender charges, unknown insurance costs, and lord knows what other charges. My first fund was advertised in Mother Jones Magazine. This nonprofit news organization specializes in investigative, political and social justice reporting. Pax World had a permanent ad in Mother Jones. This mutual fund met our values: a socially responsible fund eschewing investments in companies that purvey tobacco, weapons, drugs or harm to people or the environment. I started an IRA with Pax World. I liked the idea of investing my money in companies which share our progressive values. An IRA has the same tax advantage as the annuities – taxes are deferred until you take the money out. The application was effortless.

I stayed with them for about a year. Pax World wasn't as exciting as other funds. After one year, Pax World would make 12 percent and other funds were making 20 percent or more. So I looked for something more remunerative.

Subsequent funds I chose were often the performance leaders according to magazine or newsletter reports. I did well with these funds during the good times. I adopted the motto, "bonds are for babies" to tease Steve. This was our first inkling of philosophical differences. A few of the funds I liked were high-flyers with lots of trading within the same fund. This trading cost was another unreported expense. The managers were aggressive with occasional stellar results. But they did not last long. Greed and my budding investing self-confidence felt appropriate at the time. I wasn't concerned about high annual expenses charged by aggressive mutual fund managers as long as the returns remained high.

I found a mutual fund I liked which charged a three percent load. I asked Peter if there was any way around that. He said, "If you wouldn't mind I could be the representative," I said "No." Hmm...with the dangle of a commission in front of his face, he now works with mutual funds! For 15 years he led me to believe mutual funds were not a good idea. His conversion brings to mind the saying, "When morality comes up against profit, it's seldom that profit loses." I terminated this financial relationship. He taught me more than he intended.

Money got tight in the California State University system in 1991. The university wanted most of the job training grant money for "indirect," the word they use for management costs. There wasn't enough money left to deliver services so we parted ways.

In 1993 I was awarded a federally funded job-training grant for my new position at the Van Ness Recovery House. When I got this job I asked the director if I could start a retirement option for the employees. She told me they already had a 403(b) plan. I told her I had a better way to go. She gave the authority to inquire and initiate a new 403(b) plan.

It took two or three phone calls to get the forms and promotional materials from two well-known mutual fund companies: Fidelity Investments and T. Rowe Price. Fidelity was the largest mutual fund company at the time, rivaling Vanguard. T. Rowe Price also offered 'no load' mutual funds. It was so simple I had to crow when I got home. I knew it would never be so easy for Steve to get anything into or out of his monolithic employer. Neither of these great companies was available for Steve's 403(b).

By the middle nineties Steve and I had been together for 20 years. My investments had been aggressive during this transition while he was more cautious. I attribute that to his Midwest farm-boy reluctance to get too excited. However, we were both ready to transfer out of our annuities.

Part Two
Sprouting
Our Portfolio

CHAPTER 3

Our *Mutual* Financial Education Begins

(1 9 9 4 - 2 0 0 2)

In 1975 we were naïve investors as our individual stories show. As time passed we built on our annuity experiences and began to learn about investing for growth. We went to an investment seminar offering a neat angle for earning a consistent income leading to home ownership. This was our first prophetic mistake.

The concept was simple: invest in a factoring agreement and save the gains for a down payment on a piece of property. The investor puts money into a pot which is loaned to a large utility. This gives the company cash for anything they need. They pay the money back plus 20 percent interest.

This scheme never paid a cent. The business was shut down and the perpetrator went to jail. What were we thinking? Why would any utility consider paying so much interest?

The point is no legitimate investment can earn 12 percent, 15 percent or 20 percent year after year without market fluctuations and short-term losses. It turns out the $5,000 we lost provided a valuable lesson about 'riskless' financial gimmicks promising high rates of return in perpetuity. In this case the money didn't go anywhere but the shyster's pocket.

Steve shared his pivotal moment when that insurance agent said, "Mutual funds are too risky for teachers." This shameful reference to the entire education profession still echoes. In our opinion it's the annuity industry's equivalent to profiling—financial profiling—believing all teachers are risk averse and ignorant. How can they get away with this? No other profession allows the dominance of annuities in their retirement plans. The University of California and the California State University systems have great non-insurance, low-cost, 403(b) plans. Last we heard they are educators too.

It raises the question of how an *entire* professional pre-K-12th grade educational culture trusts their financial future to a hack in a suit sitting in the cafeteria. But almost everybody? It's hard to believe. Higher education and many public sector employees have had the low-cost TIAA CREF for almost a century. This New York not-for-profit corporation is discussed in chapter 5.

It was about this time Steve discovered his first TSA agent had ignored the specific request for a product with no surrender charges. When it was time to transfer that annuity to a mutual fund, you guessed it, it had a $2,000 surrender fee—from an $11,000 account. Does this happen because the industry feels safe to assume teachers are trusting sheep? We never again talked to another agent from an insurance company about retirement plans. The escape route was right in front of us—mutual funds.

Our lure to mutual funds became clear. Dan became leery of individual stocks, sparked by Richard Ney's *Wall Street Jungle* exposé of the Street's shenanigans. Ney outlined the problem: Wall Street opportunists, specifically the "floor specialists." These people are supposed to keep order in the market but in fact are insiders who skim profits out of most transactions, documented by Ney. The lack of meaningful enforcement means an unwary buyer is less likely to reap the full benefit of buying stocks.

Ney's solution was to predict their moves and buy sectors through Fidelity prior to their upticks. Dan subscribed to Mutual Funds, Smart Money, Forbes and other magazines in an effort to become investment savvy. Ney showed Dan how to avoid Wall Street by using mutual funds.

With the mutual funds' built-in diversification of hundreds of stocks in a single investment we don't need a professional selling us a mutual fund. Why give money to somebody who then puts it into a fund we could get ourselves? Isn't that like handing fare to a subway agent who then inserts it in the slot and gives us a ticket? Where is the added value? We have *never* regretted our decision to eschew financial advisors. For them profit trumped honest financial advice.

Mutual funds do the job of selecting investments and spreading risk across many stocks. Simple enough. We still had much to learn and were eager for the journey. We had no idea our switch from annuities to mutual funds would lead to what comes next.

Morningstar Portfolio Feature

We weren't sure how much we had accumulated until we used the Morningstar.com website to organize our holdings. After a free registration process, you click on the "Portfolio" tab, click "Create New Portfolio," enter the ticker symbols and the number of shares you own. That's it.

Morningstar has over a 100 different statistics and information on each fund, stock or bond in your portfolio. It's almost overwhelming. We discovered most of the statistics available such as alpha, beta, correlation, r-squared and book value were not useful for us (definitions are found in the Glossary). These statistics are beyond the purposes of this book and we didn't need to get caught up in all of the numerous technicalities.

The art of being wise is knowing what to overlook.

– William James

Morningstar portfolio feature shows the percentage you have in different asset classes: domestic stocks, international stocks, bonds, large company, small company stocks, cash, etc (asset classes will be discussed shortly). It shows how much your portfolio goes up or down after each trading day. It's a fantastic way to keep track of your holdings and compare them to the broad market averages.

Once you have inserted your holdings it's all automatic from then on. Morningstar adds the total, checks the current price of each share daily and multiplies it times the number of shares you own and bingo, you have a great report to print out for your records. Moreover, the site is free and easy to use.

We encouraged each other to make retirement saving a priority, cut investment costs and replace annuities with investments. Instead of giving up when Steve received the "not available" note from his employer, we charged ahead with enthusiasm and nascent confidence. And why not? By the end of 1994 we had saved about $238,000. Starting from zilch, this accomplishment took 18 years.

Our First Portfolio

Table 1 shows our portfolio at the end of 1994. About 17 percent of our nest egg came from Dan's lump-sum payout from his pension plan. The rest was from systematic monthly tax deferred payroll deductions. Dan started in May, 1976 with $100/month when he was 36 and Steve with $200 a month in January, 1985 at 37. Our employers never matched our contributions. As time passed we increased our contributions by investing half our raises and half our tax refunds.

Table 1	
Our First Portfolio, March 1994	
Aggressive Growth	
Oppenheimer Main Street	$8,555
Kaufmann	$46,000
PBHG	$4,000
Growth	
Parnassus	$9,500
Fidelity Contra	$13,618
Balanced Managed	
Fidelity Asset Manager	$13,689
Parnassus Balanced	$4,350
International	
T.R Price International Stock	$5,000
T.R. Price New Asia	$5,000
Insurance Company Annuities TSA/403b	
Great American	$20,000
Northern Life	$42,458
National Health	$10,307
National Western Life	$35,000
United Olympic	$6,500
Total with 1994 end of year contributions $15,000	$223,977 + $15,000 = $238,977

We had five annuities to transfer into stock mutual funds. We selected the funds from the year's hottest fund lists. Neither a scientific technique nor a properly diversified portfolio (as we learned later); the funds we selected were recommended by people who ought to know--financial magazine columnists, gurus, talking heads and financial conference presenters. The recommendations were made on the basis of recent performance, the size of the fund, manager tenure, and the sector. Nothing out of the ordinary--that's what many investors do.

Mutual fund companies provide IRAs which are tax-deferred. We have IRAs and an after-tax plan, Steve also has a pension. The three most popular plans are the 401(k), referring to the law governing private employer plans for their employees, the 457(b) and 403(b) for public and non-profit employees.

The Tech Bubble Begins

Talk about perfect timing. The technology bubble began its incredible growth in 1995 just after we transitioned from annuities into mutual funds. Most investors didn't know it yet but the technology stocks as a group (or 'sector') were going to multiply in value several times as it became a bubble during the next five years.

We learned later the technology bubble was no different from previous bubbles going back to the *Tulip Bubble* in 17th century Holland, the 18th century *Mississippi Scheme,* the English's South-Sea bubbles and our own well-know historical "Roaring Twenties" 1929 bubble and crash. More money was poured into technology stocks (or Tulips) than was warranted driving up their prices far exceeding their long-term prospects for *realistic* returns. We provide a glimpse of how we got caught up in the tech bubble and crash.

In 1995 and 1996 the stock market went up over 35.8 percent and 21 percent, respectively. These back to back gains were calculated from the average annual increase in the value of all stocks in the United States. Consistent growth across the board is called a Bull Market, charging ahead as it generates enthusiasm and momentum for a growing economy. Investors who seek these exciting gains put more money into the market, sometimes selling their bonds, Certificates of Deposit, bank accounts or even borrowing on their house.

Technology stocks are bought and sold through the National Association of Security Dealers Automated Quotations (NASDAQ). In 1996 the NASDAQ went up 40 percent, surpassing the overall market gain. "How wonderful," we thought at the time. The three percent performance of the fixed annuities was gone forever as we poured our money into technology sector mutual funds. What extraordinary timing, we thought.

Our portfolio reflected what was going on around the world every day *and* in *our* work environment as educators. There was a lot of media coverage about the 21st century workforce requiring computer technology skills. Our employers bought technology products. Steve accepted an out of the classroom position as technology coordinator at his elementary school. Dan wrote a grant to build a computer training class at the Van Ness Recovery House in Hollywood, where he worked as a job trainer. We were confident we knew enough about the technology companies and the ensuing expansion to channel our investing. How could we go wrong? We lived and worked right in the middle of the technology revolution. Our confidence went *up* higher than the booming stock market. Our fear of risk disappeared like prairie dogs to the hungry coyote's encroachment.

Los Angeles Times' *Money Makeover*

In 1996 the Los Angeles Times launched a Money Makeover segment. The reporters featured stories of people's financial circumstances and their investments. A financial professional was asked by the Times to look at the holdings and offer recommendations with the results presented in a detailed article. This great learning tool continues to this day.

After several years without a financial adviser Steve wondered what a professional might say about our holdings. "After all, it's free," Steve thought. On a hunch he submitted our portfolio information to the Money Makeover editor. We were accepted as the first gay couple. Table 2 shows what we submitted to the Los Angeles Times.

Table 2
Portfolio Sent to Los Angeles Times 12/1996

Mutual Fund	Ticker	Amount
Fidelity Select Electronics	FSELX	$33,978
Fidelity Select Computers	FDCPX	$11,981
Fidelity New Millennium	FMILX	$29,899
Fidelity Dividend Growth	FDGFX	$21,995
Fidelity Select Consumer Fin.	FSVLX	$24,996
Fidelity Contra Fund	FCNTX	$7,598
Fidelity Mid-Cap Fund	FMCXS	$39,926
Fidelity Equity Income II	FEQTX	$12,445
INVESCO Equity Income	FIIIX	$5,680
INVESCO Financial Services	FSFSX	$5,065
INVESCO Health Services	FHLSX	$4,547
INVESCO Technology	FTCHX	$14,062
T. R. Price Health Services	PRHSX	$837
T. R. Price America Growth	PRWAX	$1,569
T. R. Price Science &Technology	PRSCX	$771
T. R. Price New Horizens	PRNHX	$16,243
PBHG Core Growth	PBCRX	$7,524
PBHG Emerging Growth	PBEGX	$5,099
PBHG Funds	PBTCX	$20,373
PBHG Growth	PBHGX	$54,263
PBHG Select Equity	PBHEX	$33,002
Federated Kaufman	KAUFX	60,039
Mairs & Power Growth	MPGFX	10,977
Oakmark Small Cap	OAKSX	$27,799
	Total	**$450,668**

Total Stock Market Index Returned 23 percent and
NASDAQ gained almost 40 percent in 1996.

The advisor recommended bonds and broader diversification. We figured we were already diversified with many mutual fund holdings. We told ourselves "our risk is spread over hundreds of technology companies. We want growth and lots of it; we're too young to worry about the balance between bonds and stocks." We didn't listen to his sound advice. After all, isn't the goal to accumulate money and not a bunch of conservative bonds or those broadly diversified passé mutual funds?

Our risk tolerance was tested on October 27, 1997. We recall how pleased we were with our ongoing success. Steve wrote in his journal, *"The Dow plunged 554 points and the NASDAQ lost 115 points. Neither Dan nor I had this kind of loss before. Our portfolio lost about $38,000 today and it's down to $550,000 from a high of $620,000 a couple of weeks ago. That is a loss of $70,000. This is a lot of money, but we are hanging in there as usual."* We didn't panic.

OMG

On November 11, 1999, our portfolio topped $1 million. It closed at $1,000,104.00, up $12,500 on that happy day. Our friend Brad left a phone message, "Hello Millionaires" and congratulated us. We were thrilled. Whether it was five years earlier when we took charge of our investing or 24 years earlier when we started out, we never imagined this kind of tremendous growth coming to fruition. Perhaps our heads swelled a little (or maybe a lot). But *more* growth is coming.

The Remarkable Winter of 1999-2000:
$500,000 growth in Four Months.

Talk about being in the middle of the sweet spot of stock market history, what more can we report? In 1999 the major market averages, the Dow Jones Industrial Average and the NASDAQ soared once again.

The Dow is another one of the publicized indicators of the nation's economic health. In three and a half years the Dow had doubled from 5,000 in November, 1995 to 10,006 on March 30, 1999 topping 10,000 for the first time in history. To say 1999 and the turn of the century was a remarkable economic and political time for our country would be an understatement. Optimism was everywhere--President Clinton's media-blitzed impeachment trial was a non-issue as far as stock market performance was concerned.

Business and mainstream financial media repeated ad nauseam "this time is different." The peace-dividend from the end of the 40-year cold war was real. Instead of using our collective talent to build expensive weapons, we created and manufactured consumer goods which improved our living and working lives. What a novel idea. There was full employment and millions of mainstream workers invested in the stock market for the first time. Corporations made big profits. Analysts reported technology created a huge leap to improved workplace production efficiency and reduced costs.

Intel, Applied Materials, Cisco Systems and Microsoft made oodles of money selling their popular electronic gadgets which sent their stocks higher. Computer chips were manufactured by Applied Materials and Intel. The infrastructure of the Internet was reflected in Cisco Systems. Software applications and operating systems were developed and sold by Microsoft.

We bought United Parcel Service (UPS) believing home delivery services would grow symbiotically. At the time Internet commerce and delivery systems were expanding--even grocery orders could be handled online. The remainder of our stock holdings were speculative: Catalyst Semiconductor, Netcreations, Sonic Wall, ACTV, and Kinetics. They were typical dot com companies recommended by our niece who worked for Schwab. They also doubled in price. The pharmaceutical giant Pfizer was recommended by a friend who worked for the company and was expecting spectacular gains. We liked the name too... sounded like a good name for a dog.

Pay Off the Mortgage?

Dan proposed paying off the mortgage of $78,000 but Steve said we would have to sell shares and pay capital gains taxes. It seemed silly with an already low interest rate on the mortgage. Wouldn't it be dumb to pull money out of the market when it was earning more than the interest we were paying on our mortgage? Well, duh…the stock returns were paying a lot more. Dan agreed.

We believed we had those gains in our pockets.

We fancied ourselves as potential eleemosynaries. A wonderful thought, though premature. We weren't taking money out.

Alan Greenspan, the Federal Reserve Chairman, lauded the days of deregulation but also made his infamous quip "irrational exuberance" referring to the soaring stock market. The most surprising positive economic indicator was the politically implausible federal budget surplus. Nineteen sixty-nine was the only other year the federal budget produced a surplus in our lifetimes. This news was so good some economic prognosticators said the total accumulated national debt of six trillion dollars could be paid off by 2010.

The technology sector did so well, sometimes our portfolio gained *or* lost $35,000 to $70,000 in a single-day trading session. All of this was exciting and fascinating. We were awed with the daily movements exceeding our annual salaries. Charles Mackay wrote in his famous book, *Extraordinary Popular Delusions & the Madness of Crowds,* in 1841, "…in the course of a few hours, and many persons in the humble walks of life who had risen poor in the morning, went to bed in affluence." That's us. Isn't this how investments are supposed to work?

Winter was freezing as technology sizzled. The winter of 1999-2000 will go down in stock market history as yielding the greatest gain in the shortest period. Our portfolio followed the technology sector point for point. It took us 22 years to build our wealth from zero to

$500,000, another four years to grow to $1 million but only four months to grow another half million. We were convinced investments worked this way.

The final $500,000 growth occurred from November 11, 1999 to March 10, 2000, an average of $6,000 higher per trading day during that winter. Table 3 shows our Morningstar.com printout for March 3, 2000. A week later, Steve wrote in his journal our portfolio edged over $1.5 million. The NASDAQ reached its all-time high of 5132.52 on Friday March 10, 2000, the highest in its 40-year history.

The Dow and another frequently reported economic gauge, the S&P 500 Index, were showing signs of leveling off and letting the NASDAQ go its own way. They dropped that day and for the week.

Wall Street and the financial media spin machines were overwhelmingly optimistic. Chief technical analyst for Prudential Securities, Ralph Acampora, predicted the NASDAQ would hit 6,000 before the end of 2001. James Glassman and Kevin Hassett predicted the Dow would reach 36,000 in their 1999 book, *Dow 36,000*. Many financial analysts and media pundits repeated this mantra. The market was poised to continue going up with occasional declines, blah, blah, blah. When will it end?

Table 3
Portfolio on March 3, 2000

Name	Ticker	Amount
Applied Materials	AMAT	$19,075
Artisan International	ARTIX	34,357
Cash		2,000
Catalyst Semiconductor Inc	CATS	5,453
Cisco Systems	CSCO	68,718
CTS Corporation	CTS	2,615
Fidelity New Millennium	FMILX	155,895
Fidelity Select Electronics	FSELX	115,506
Fidelity Select Computers	FDCPX	57,342
ACTV Inc.	ISTV	6,950
INVESCO Worldwide Telecom	ISWCX	27,257
Intel Corporation	INTC	31,005
Janus Balanced	JABAX	25,039
Janus Global Lifescience	JAGLX	130,545
Janus Enterprise	JAENX	61,674
Janus Global Technology	JAGTX	136,172
Janus Mercury	JAMRX	20,690
Janus Twenty	JAVLX	10,927
Kinetiks.com	KNET	1,763
Minnesota Mining & Mfg	MMM	2,238
Microsoft	MSFT	38,450
NTN Communications	NTN	1,219
Net creations Inc	NTCR	5,400
Pfizer Corp.	PFE	9,787
Red Oak Technology Select	ROGSX	63,756
Pin Oak Aggressive Stock	POGSX	50,796
Sonic Wall Inc.	SNWL	10,400
Firsthand Technology Value	TVFQX	92,652
United Parcel Services, INC	UPS	2,634
Vanguard Capital Opportunity	VHCOX	153,025
Vanguard 500 Index	VFINX	16,532
Vanguard Asset Allocation	VAAPX	21,381
Vanguard Total Stock Mkt Indx	VTSMX	5,914
Vanguard U.S. Growth	VWUSX	1,422
Vanguard GNMA	VFIIX	55,421
White Oak Select Growth	WOGSX	6,318
3-March-2000	Total	$1,450,328

Dan had been nagging Steve for months to trade our last bond fund in his 403(b). Because of the tremendous gains Steve missed in the last year, he agreed to buy yet another technology fund. Steve executed his $55,000 trade in March, 2000.

Not Only Us

Looking back at our portfolio with 90 percent invested in tech stocks, we felt secure. It never occurred to us we were obsessed with technology company stocks. *Everybody* was doing it—the professionals, too. We were no different from millions of other investors who eschewed balance, value, and diverse investments in favor of marvelous hype and rationalization. We thought we were OK when investors who follow Warren Buffet's Berkshire Hathaway lost money as everybody else seemed to be getting richer.

"Turn out the Lights, the Party's Over…."

If you are an investor and lived through the dot com bubble you know what happened. After five years the tiny bubble became a hot air balloon and popped. This sector began its downward trend on March 10, 2000. By June our portfolio lost $400,000. It regained $200,000 after a summer rally. We tried to feel comfortable. The markets go up and down and we always thought long-term, but we never expected this tremendous volatility. The news never mentioned the economy might be heading into a recession. "A momentary blip," we rationalized.

Before the outpouring of your smug schadenfreude

oozes: yes, we were dumb. For us it was perfectly sane. We aren't keen on taking full responsibility so we put as much blame on the financial experts as we can get away with. An excellent example is the expert who predicted the NASDAQ would go to 6,000, optimism gone awry, reflecting the "recency effect"- a powerful psychological effect of our human tendency to infer the recent stock market momentum will continue its upward trend.

It's expected that we would fall victim, but how could so many professionals have predicted such irresistible stupidity? Very simply. David Denby wrote in his book about his personal experience interviewing the principals of Wall Street during the tech bubble crash, *American Sucker:* "There is no gain in ever saying, 'sell this stock.'" If an analyst, manager, or economist worth their beans predicted at any conference, meeting or interview the NASDAQ might retreat from 5132 to a low of 1114 in 2002, they would have been demoted, fired *and* burned at the stake.

Why don't active managers whose major sales pitch is to get investors out safely before a bear market fail so miserably? Jeremy Grantham (Co-founder of Boston Investment Firm, GMO) says, "The best way… to reduce your career and business risk is to make sure you're doing whatever everyone else is doing. You look around [at what other managers] are saying and doing, and you…fit into the pack. Now if you are wrong, that is not a significant reason to get fired" (quoted in Braham). Grantham added every manager he surveyed knew the bubble was about to burst, but didn't get out because they feared they would lag behind their peers and get fired.

The technology bubble evaporated further in concert with the tragic events of 9/11 and subsequent yearlong geopolitical risks. The stock market hit bottom by the fall of 2002. We didn't panic in the wake of the wars in the Middle East sans budget or method of payment, leading to massive uncertainty and fear in the country.

Our portfolio gains from 1995-2000 vanished— over a million dollars. Still, we asked ourselves how could the glory days of the nineties disappear so fast?

In his book, *Your Money and Your Mind,* Jason Zweig's documented part of our story. We watched with great pain as our portfolio sank lower and lower. Zweig quoted Dan's reflection on this calamity, "I felt like this dog I'd seen once in the middle lane of an L.A. freeway in the rain. It had been grazed by a car and looked into the oncoming traffic with this kind of pained smile, like it was thinking, "It doesn't matter whether you hit me or whether you miss me all I know is I can't run anymore." And Dan said to himself, "That's you, Dan. You're just like the dog you saw in the rain." What more bad news could we endure? One more crisis blindsided both of us.

During a routine medical exam on a hot Friday afternoon August 18, 2000, Steve was diagnosed with cancer requiring surgery. The following Tuesday his 91 year-old mother died. She was buried on a Monday in Wisconsin. Steve was on the operating table back in Los Angeles the following Friday.

Our chief concern was Steve's health. The surgery was routine but recovery painful, slow and debilitating. For the next four years Steve had routine checkups to see if the cancer had spread. Through it all he continued to contribute to his 403(b). He went back to school at age 53 to earn an administrative credential and accepted a five-year, part-time position at UCLA Extension teaching educational technology.

We knew enough about investing to realize it's not wise to sell during the middle of a crisis. We are "buy and hold" types.

We made three primary mistakes, one psychological and two strategic:

1. We were overconfident, too excited and, yes, greedy.
2. We had not diversified our holdings among other types of stocks including international funds nor a variety of bonds.
3. We failed to recognize the bubble because we were certain this time was different.

Our mistakes are common among new investors who get lucky right-out-of-the-gate in a huge way, like the few slot-pulling seniors at the casinos or the majority of lottery winners, only to lose it all. We didn't know enough about bubbles. We thought we were different, we had the touch; anointed, in a way.

Had we become two little clones of our former financial advisers? Greedy in the up market and quiet as the sector tumbled? Those media pundits changed their tune and abandoned tech recommendations for rock-solid companies with good balance sheets and earnings. It didn't matter to them. The industry makes money whether the market goes up or down. The tech bubble became an event of the distant past. Old news is about as useful and current as yesterday's newspaper blowing down an alley.

We couldn't forget. The greed label hit us hard when our investing decisions went wrong. If $1.5 million isn't enough in the first place, what possessed us to hang on, hoping for a recovery? We were in shock and stopped looking at the market and refused to sell at the bottom.

Our previous losses hadn't been so bad: the Asian Contagion in 1997 and the back-to-back collapses in 1998: the Russian Sovereign Default leading to the collapse of the American hedge fund Long-Term Capital Management. These examples tested our risk tolerance and we passed because the markets recovered in a few short months, no big deal. But the dot com crash almost proved fatal, in fact, the technology sector still has not recovered. Cisco Systems stock price remains the same in 2012 as it was in 1998. The NASDAQ hasn't recovered anywhere near its historic high.

We began to shift our thinking to engage in the complexity of middle-ground investing. The vicissitudes of the market are not designed for stability but rather to encourage frequent buying and selling. This discontent with the promotional part of the financial industry but not with the entire range of stocks themselves was one of the lessons we learned.

Our portfolio declined to where we began in 1996--$460,000! We wondered long and hard how hundreds of technology company stocks in our mutual funds could fall all at once. To use the standard cliché and ask the question, were "all of our eggs in the same basket?" Did we have pseudo diversification? One prolonged reflective moment after another we ended up with the identical question, if what we had wasn't diversification what is valid diversification?

Still, monetary losses pale in comparison to a life threatening disease. The cancer had not metastasized. Follow-up tests showed the treatment was 100 percent effective. Those years 2000 to 2002 were tough and challenging financially, emotionally and physically.

Regardless of the amount of money involved, whether $1.5 million or $460,000, what difference does that really make? A deadly disease diagnosis guarantees anyone into a life-affirming perspective. As Steve put it, "my life and our life together are as strong as ever, and for that we are both grateful."

CHAPTER 4

Back to Basics

(2 0 0 3)

The tech bubble and cancer got our attention. With retirement imminent we could not afford to waste time commiserating. Our mistakes were not unique but were expensive. Losing a million dollars and Steve's health required a major look at our values and priorities. There were two great lessons: impermanence and gratitude. Crises and bubbles come and go but stock market uncertainty lives on.

During our darkest days we knew bear markets return to profitability. That's part of investing. In any given 30-year period since 1928 the overall stock market returned an average of about 8 percent a year. Eight percent return is good but it's an *average*. It doesn't hold true for all individual stocks or asset classes nor does the return go up eight percent every year.

How could we smooth out the unpredictability of

individual stocks and sector funds? We embarked on a review of the basics. In order to capture an optimal realistic return of the stock market we needed a less risky approach. We drew closer to the mutual fund concept. Just as we thought we had diversification within the tech stocks we started to look at a larger domain of stocks and bonds.

Recall, the L.A. Times adviser recommended a balanced approach with all investments. This led us to the following questions:

1. How is the stock market organized so we can construct a genuine diversified portfolio?
2. What is an IPO?
3. What is market capitalization?
4. What determines trading costs?
5. What are the major domestic and international asset classes?
6. How do stock and bond diversification mitigate risk?
7. What are the different types of bonds?
8. How can everyday investors protect assets from crashes?

We began our search for the pieces necessary to build a new strategy designed to protect our portfolio from another 70 percent loss heading into retirement. This required a deeper understanding of market fundamentals. If you are a newbie investor, this chapter shows what we discovered and what you should know.

The Stock Market

The stock market raises money for corporate America by selling shares of stocks (aka equities), a small piece of the company. It's an opportunity for all of us to participate in the growth of companies and the economy. Pension plans, institutional investors for universities and states and other governments also invest in our economy. That's how it's supposed to work.

How is the Stock Market organized?

Charles Dow, a journalist, created a chart to monitor the progress of the stock market over time and make sense of the confusion it often produced. He created the Dow Jones Industrial Average, the "Dow," in 1896. In order to comprehend overall market trends with a consistent measuring tool he tracked 12 representative stocks (10 railroads and two industrials).

Over the years the Dow has expanded to 30 large companies. They represent a cross section of businesses. Steve's mom was invested in one of those companies, 3M, one of the oldest members of the Dow. It's part of the manufacturing sector of the stock market. Other companies in the Dow represent gas and oil, pharmaceuticals, financial and retail companies.

The Dow number represents the average of the 30 corporations' stock prices. This average is derived from the daily overall gain or loss in value. It's not important to know the calculation for our purposes, but it's a snapshot of how the economy and the stock market are performing.

Millions of Businesses

The United States has millions of corporations, companies, farms, ranches, boutiques and convenience stores, according to the U.S. Census Bureau. The Small Business Administration reports there are more than 27 million businesses alone. Most are tiny companies which do not have employees. Only a tiny fraction offer shares. 3M and more than 5,000 other companies sell shares to investors as "publicly traded companies." An additional 2,000 companies trade shares but are too small to be included in the daily reports. A few companies grow into large companies. When large companies' sales are slow, hundreds of their suppliers are negatively affected too. Thus a small number of large corporations wield a large economic influence on the entire economy.

People who monitor the market on a daily basis look at the performance of the Dow and other exchanges as benchmarks to see how the day, the quarter or year went. A huge amount of past data is available.

The three major exchanges in the United States are:

- New York Stock Market Exchange (NYSE) with 1666 companies listed
- National Association of Securities Dealers Automatic Quote (NASDAQ), with 3,015 companies
- American Stock Exchange (AMEX), with 375 companies

These exchanges are the physical and virtual space

where shares of 3M and the other 5,055 companies are traded in the open market.

Initial Public Offering

Sometimes a company does so well it needs money to grow. How do they raise money? Issuing stock and "going public" invites investors to own part of the business. After a company secures the approval of the Securities and Exchange Commission's (SEC) regulators to sell shares an Initial Public Offering (IPO) is issued to the public. From then on it's called a publicly traded company and new shares are sold. The SEC monitors the stock trading.

IPO money raised by selling stock allows them to purchase equipment, hire new employees and grow the company. Ordinary investors may realize short-term IPO gains but it's not worth the risk, in our opinion. The primary initial gains are collected by preferred customers of the Wall Street brokers and bankers handling the deal (e.g., Facebook).

As a 3M shareholder Steve has certain rights. He receives information about the annual shareholder meetings and can vote his proxy on issues which affect the corporation as a whole. The primary concern of the shareholder is to make sure the assets grow to meet retirement goals.

As with any piece of property the seller and buyer determines the price of a share. It's nothing complicated, both agree on a price and a trade is completed. When more investors sell shares of a company than are bought, the price declines. Sales produce commissions and possible benefit from the difference between the buying and selling prices called a "spread." One of the dirty little secrets of the spread is that sellers obtain the lower selling price and buyers pay the higher buying price. Ney documents that stockbrokers and commissioned-based advisers pocket the "spread" difference for profits. With computerized trading the benefit from a fraction of a cent difference can be huge with a large volume of shares.

One approach to circumvent this cost is to avoid individual stocks and to limit trading activity. We focused on asset classes. When we discovered these broad classes we realized how groups of investments could work for us for a change.

Asset Classes:
Capitalization, Domestic and International

The stock market contains millions of shares offered by thousands of publicly traded companies. With so much information to digest, how can we decide which company to invest in? Isn't choosing among all these shares and thousands of different companies more complicated than buying a car? Yes. But Wall Street addresses this complication by classifying groups of companies into asset classes and reducing thousands of stocks down to a group of five or six core classes of stocks.

One of the best ideas we have learned from reading and talking with investors is to use these grouped categories--the broadest asset classes available. How? During the bubble our portfolio was limited to large tech stocks. To our chagrin we discovered investing in one sector was too narrow. The fall in value of the sector was similar to inexorable losses in an individual company stock. In his book, *The Power of Passive Investing*, Rick Ferri describes this particular risk exactly: "Market risk is risk of the entire asset class. It cannot be diversified away by adding more securities [or tech stocks] or the same asset class [or sector] into a portfolio."

The Standard and Poor's (S&P 500) Index represents the largest companies--traced back to 1860 when William Poor published his comprehensive book about the financial and operational systems in the United States stock market. The size of each of those 500 companies gives them weight in the calculation of the index. Large cap is an abbreviation for large capitalization. Capitalization is calculated by multiplying the number of a company's shares outstanding by its stock price per share. The "outstanding" shares are held by investors.

Apple is the largest American corporation measured by the biggest market capitalization (September, 2012). Exxon is second. Along with 3M, these are included in the S&P 500. The following three major indices provide size guidelines for the five thousand stock offerings:

- **Large Cap (Capitalization) Index:** the S&P 500 Index Companies worth more than $10 billion.

- **Mid Cap:** $1 billion to $10 billion

- **Small Cap:** $100 million to $1 billion

Another way to view the 5,000 major companies is to know there are about 500 large-cap, 500 mid-cap, and 2,000 small cap companies. The remaining companies have smaller capitalizations and are not counted in the major asset classes. The companies in the indices are selected by a Wall Street committee to see if aspiring companies grow big enough (or shrink) in their capitalization for inclusion (or removal) in one of the three major asset classes.

The total worth of each company determines which of the three asset classes it belongs to. 3M has about 715 million shares owned by individual investors and institutions (pensions, mutual funds, and hedge funds) all over the world. As mentioned each share costs $86.24 (April 2012). Multiply 715 million total shares by the price: 715,000,000 x $86.24 = about $60 billion of capitalization.

3M has sufficient value to qualify as a large-cap. Of the 500 large-cap companies, 3M is one company. When we invest in the S&P 500 large cap index, we own Apple, Exxon, 3M and 497 other large cap companies (Table 4). This is one core fund for diversification.

After the Dow Jones Industrial Average (DJIA), the S&P 500 is a universally followed index of large-cap American stocks. It gives a picture of the broad economy since it measures 500 businesses, including the 30 in the DJIA. The DJIA industrials are too few to qualify as an asset class, in our opinion.

Categorizing companies by size permits us to buy a handy basket of companies' stock in a single index.

Steve Schullo and Dan Robertson

An investor who's only interested in large stocks will purchase a large-cap index. Why? Large-cap companies do more extensive business overseas with a broader scope of sales and earnings than small-cap companies. This sounds good, but this particular investor will miss out on the potential returns of mid- and small-cap companies. Large-cap is one asset class. We're talking about *three* U.S.-based asset classes. We want to invest in *all* available asset classes for broad diversification.

Small-caps are riskier than large cap companies but tend to have greater long-term growth. Their values can fluctuate in the short term but potential returns can be attractive when held for many years.

Each asset class changes as some companies' capitalization changes or--as in the Enron bankruptcy case--they're removed from the asset class and from the stock market. Fortunately, bankruptcies and capitalization adjustments have minimal effects on the entire index because of the built-in diversification of many companies over different industries.

Hundreds of technology companies in a sector mutual fund are not diversified because of the single industry focus—we won't make that pseudo diversification mistake again. We discovered that the broadest asset classes are de facto proper diversification and comprise an essential part of our new strategy. This was a huge development and turning point in our learning process.

Table 4 shows each asset class with sample mutual funds which track each class.

Table 4
United States Domestic Stock Market Asset Classes

Large-Cap 500 Companies	Mid-Cap 500 Companies	Small-Cap 2000 Companies
Largest Companies	Next Largest 501-1000	Small Companies 1001-3000
Top Holdings: Exxon Apple 3M (60th in Index)	Top Holdings: H.J. Heinz Avon Products Abercrombie & Fitch	Top Holdings: Tupperware 3COM E-TRADE
(Invests in the large-cap 500 companies) 1. Fidelity Spartan S&P 500 Index 2. Vanguard S&P 500 Index	(Invests in Mid-Cap companies) *Vanguard Mid-Cap Index*	(Invests in Small-Cap companies) *1. Vanguard Small-Cap Index 2. Fidelity Small-Cap Enhanced Index*

Top Holdings: 3M (60th in Index)

| | Below are the indexes which invest in the Mid-Cap and Small-Cap companies combined: *1. Vanguard Extended Market Index 2. Fidelity Spartan Extended Market Index* ||

Below are the Indexes which track and Invest in <u>all</u> three of the above columns: Large, Mid and Small-Cap Companies:
1. *Vanguard Total Stock Market Index*
2. *TIAA-CREF Equity Index*
3. *Fidelity Spartan Total Market Index Fund*

There is more diversification available. Consider half of the earnings received by the top 500 companies come from overseas. It might make you reflect on the growing economic force of international markets and the global economy at work. They are larger than U.S. markets, have different opportunities, and become attractive as this economy struggles. Think bigger.

The World Stock Market

Table 5 illustrates the international and global stock market asset classes. The two primary classes for foreign investments are developed markets and emerging markets. **International** mutual funds own hundreds of overseas stocks *excluding* the United States. **Global** funds own many of the available publicly traded companies in the world *including* the United States.

The bottom of Table 5 shows sample investment mutual funds to consider for international diversification.

Table 5
International/Global Stock Market Asset Classes

Developed Markets	Emerging Markets (Developing countries)
Australia Greece New Zealand Hong Kong Norway Austria Iceland Portugal Belgium Ireland Singapore Canada Israel Spain Cyprus Italy Sweden Denmark Japan Switzerland Finland France Luxembourg United Kingdom Germany Netherlands United States*	Brazil South Africa China South Korea Egypt Turkey India Indonesia Mexico Philippines Poland Russia
Invests in Developed Market countries only: • *Vanguard Developed Markets Index* • *TIAA-CREF International Equities Index* • *Fidelity Spartan International Enhanced Index*	Invests in Emerging Market countries only: • *Vanguard Emerging Market Stock Index* • *TIAA-CREF Emerging Market Equity Index* • *Fidelity Spartan Emerging Markets Index Fund*
Invests in both Developed Markets and Emerging Markets (Excluding U.S.) • *Vanguard Total International Stock Index* • *Vanguard FTSE All World ex-U.S. Index*	
Invests in the entire planetary economies: United States, Developed and Emerging Markets • *TIAA CREF Global Equities* • *Vanguard Total World Stock Market Index*	

Diversification and Risk

Our investment skills took on an edge of renewed excitement. We discovered we could invest in mainstream funds which offer diversified positions in domestic and foreign stocks. Each asset class has gains and losses, not always at the same time. Bonds also have various levels of risk but are less risky than stocks. The advantage of a balance of equities and bonds which increase or decrease at different rates is that over time there is steady growth. We have always expected some economic drama, up or down, but now aim for a comfortable balance.

The Bond Market

A bond can be issued by a corporation to raise money. Instead of the bond holder owning part of the company the investor lends money to the corporation. In return he or she gets a yield or interest payment plus the face value of the bond at the end (or maturity date) of the bond agreement. The bond market is worth about $30 trillion.

Table 6 shows how the bond market is categorized. We invest in government bonds and corporate bonds. International and municipal bonds are also valid options for diversification. Foreign bond funds charge two to three times more in annual expenses than domestic bond funds. With the recent small amount of yield from bonds we prefer to maximize our gains by avoiding those higher costs. Until the industry reduces the foreign bond fund costs, we are staying with domestic bonds.

Table 6
Bond Market

Treasury Issues backed by the U.S. Treasury	Government Sponsored Entities (GSE) Mortgaged Back Securities (MBS)	Corporate Bonds	Municipal Bonds ("Munis") Local or state sponsored Most are tax-exempt	International Bonds
Treasury Bills (T-bills) Treasury Notes (T-Notes)	Government National Mortgage Association (GNMA, pronounced Ginnie Mae).	Investment Grade Bonds (Rated higher than Junk Bonds)	Locally issued by hundreds of thousands of state and local municip-alities	Emerging Market Bonds Developed Market Bonds
Treasury Bonds (T-Bonds)	National Mortgage Association (Fannie Mae)	High-Yield Bonds are also called *Junk Bonds.*		
Treasury Inflation Protectio n (TIPS) & IBonds	Federal Home Loan Mortgage Corp. (Freddie Mac)	(Rated BBB or below)		

A bond is one of the most common investments people consider safe. We have heard all our lives, "Invest in America. Buy US Savings Bonds" or buy "War Bonds" extolled by FDR to fund World War II. Table 6 illustrates the generic names of familiar bonds.

There are $8 trillion on the sidelines (cash deposits, money markets, etc.) waiting to be invested in safe and decent returns when the economy improves. With local, national, and international debt pretty much out of control, reinvesting will be as difficult as getting water out of an already squeezed sponge.

Not all bonds fit every need. A muni, short for municipal bond, is issued by local municipality or state project. Most are federal and state tax exempt. You'll get a smaller rate of interest but it's tax-free, attractive to high net-worth individuals as a hedge against taxes. Risky munis pay more interest to entice buyers. Some have high credit risk (risk of default) due to the economic slowdown and tight budgets of many local governments. Foreign and muni bonds add diversification within your bond holding, but we don't own them at this time.

Instead we own Inflation Protected Treasuries (TIPS) which pay low interest but add the rate of inflation to the value of the bonds. When the official inflation rate is three percent the TIPS keep up with inflation while a non-TIPS bond paying less than inflation falls behind. For example, a non-TIPS bond paying two percent is losing one percent in buying power when inflation hovers at three percent.

Whenever the market gets scary you'll see a rush to gold and TIPS to obtain inflation protection. It's nice to see *something* go up when bad economic news dampens prospects. TIPS mitigate some of the effects of inflation.

We are not bond experts nor do we aspire to be. We are presenting what we have learned and done as a result of careful study and what works for us. We chose bonds to protect our portfolio from significant downside risk and to provide retirement income. If you wish to know more, there are many excellent books written about bonds. One personal favorite is *The Guide to a Winning Bond Strategy* by Larry Swedroe.

Although investing in a bond fund means we can get low cost bond services without the paperwork or trips to the bank and complicated tax reporting, it's still important to check out the types of bonds and ratings before you purchase a bond fund.

No magic formula predicts how a basket of bonds will do. For example, you might have a delightful clutch of high-rated bonds in a fund paying mucho bucks. When new bonds are issued paying higher rates, other investors may dump the former bonds to chase the new higher interest rate. Your bonds become less valuable since the "hot money" goes elsewhere. The point is to seek the highest rated short term and some medium term duration bonds that are diversified in a balanced plan which is monitored by bond experts in a reputable low-cost fund. This smoothes the rough spots and allows us all to sleep comfy.

Table 7 shows how bonds are rated. It's easy to see the ratings of a fund you want. Enter the five-letter ticker symbol into Yahoo Finance. This site lists the major bond holdings and the percentage rated AA or BBB, etc. We look for an average rating of A or higher.

Table 7
Credit Quality: Rating of Bonds for Risk of Default

AA or AAA: Highest Ratings, lowest risk

Less than AA but higher than B: Medium risk

Less than BBB: Highest risk of default

As with the equity portion of our portfolio we reduce risk by diversifying into various bond funds. Bonds are historically less volatile than equities but they sometimes outshine stocks, especially in a down year for equities (e.g., 2008). Still they have risks: the price or the value fluctuates as a direct result of interest rate adjustments by the government or the marketplace. As a rule, as risk goes up so does the return. How do we know the prospects of getting our principle back along with a good rate of interest? We use low-cost reputable bond funds.

Bond Funds vs. Individual Bonds

Table 8 shows our bond holdings. It shows the names of the fund companies we use--Vanguard and Loomis Sayles. Ninety-nine percent of our bonds are in these fund families. Most major mutual fund companies have bond funds available.

We choose Vanguard and Loomis because their costs are low, have skilled management and can provide monthly income during the distribution phase of retirement. Once the accounts are set up between our credit union and Vanguard (and Dan's Loomis Sayles

Bond Fund) the distributions are automatically sent to our checking accounts.

Table 8: Bond Funds We Own			
U.S. Treasuries	Mortgage Backed	Corporate	Municipal and International
1. Vanguard Short-Term Treasuries. 2. Vanguard Intermediate-Term Treasuries 3. Vanguard TIPs 4. Treasurydirect.gov iBond	Government National Mortgage Association: 1. Vanguard GNMA Aka Ginnie Maes	1. Vanguard Intermediate-Term Investment-Grade 2. Loomis-Sayles	Neither munis nor international bonds are necessary for our portfolio at this time due to high costs.
We own this fund: **Vanguard Total Bond Market Index** (This single fund contains 1/3 Treasuries, 1/3 GNMAs and 1/3 Corporate). It's an excellent diversified fund.			

Steve and his mom purchased individual federal bonds. When Steve sold his bonds at maturity he had to go to his bank and then decide what to do with the money. Good grief! Steve didn't want to go through that on a regular basis. Today it's easier.

You can purchase bonds from treasurydirect.gov. The Treasury Direct website provides excellent information about government bonds. At this time Treasury Direct bonds are not available through your employer-sponsored tax-deferred retirement plan.

The Vanguard Total Bond Market fund contains several different types of bonds: Treasuries, Ginnie Maes and corporate.

Using Bonds to Rebalance

Why are bonds essential to any portfolio? For these reasons: diversification (balance), safety from a crash, getting regular income in retirement, preservation of capital (keeping the money in a safe place) and to rebalance the portfolio.

Bonds are crucial for mitigating risk for the entire portfolio. The higher the proportion of stocks to bonds the greater the risk of volatility (and loss) within the portfolio. More bonds than stocks lower volatility which is appropriate for us older folks.

Younger investors can afford and need the equity risk which comes with a higher proportion of stocks to bonds. Over time they should have a larger overall final result as they accept risk in the early years.

As we get older this ratio reverses. We protect our nest egg by becoming progressively conservative to minimize risk and invest for retirement income. This approach uses the early investing years for growth with an emphasis on stock funds. We increase bonds and income funds as we approach retirement. Target Retirement funds do this automatically and are discussed in chapter ten.

We are almost ready to put our plan together. But first we need to review what we know so far, combined into a practical financial point of view—a philosophy of investing.

CHAPTER 5

Late-Bloomer's Portfolio Evolution

(2 0 0 4 - 2 0 0 7)

Good news flourished from the 2003 stock market returns.

With a portfolio which grew 35 percent from the bubble low we felt damn good. Our tech-heavy portfolio bounced back from a low of $460,000 in October, 2002 up 35 percent by January, 2004—in fourteen months the portfolio grew to $622,000. What happened? Underneath the doom and gloom, markets do what they have always done after a prolonged bear market. Suddenly, they become bull markets.

Steve continued his 403(b) contributions and Dan started receiving Social Security in 2003. It was a great year for major market averages: the Dow was up 25.3 percent, the S&P 500 gained 26.4 percent and the NASDAQ jumped 50.0 percent. It was a marvelous reprieve yet we felt chastened and eager to put our financial house in order. Our goal was to build an investment strategy which could perform in any market climate: diversified and reflecting the core asset classes discussed in the previous chapter.

Dan (63) had already retired and Steve (57) was four years away. It was essential to avoid annuities and bubble chasing. We didn't know which specific mutual funds we wanted to transfer into, because we were starting over. This was a tall order. It didn't happen overnight. We knew we had to get out of our tech heavy portfolio *ASAP.*

The Transition Begins

Steve learned from reading in the Bogleheads investment forum that earning the average return of the whole market provides a middle ground: less volatility, less risk, better sleep. This idea of average returns didn't appeal to Dan until he learned market average gains are higher than managed funds 80 percent of the time. The asset classes and bonds provide the positive cornerstones of our new approach.

Our search began with a guiding philosophy—John Bogle's work with the Vanguard Group. We needed to clarify: (1) our active/passive strategy debate, (2) excessive trading and costs, and (3) speculation vs. usual risk.

Eureka! The Man Who Created Index Funds

Steve found his epiphany at the popular Bogleheads. org investment forum and in John Bogle's books about index funds. This forum includes many savvy and gratis contributors committed to balanced investing and indexing. It's rare to find free unbiased resource where real people answer your specific financial questions.

Affectionately titled "St. Jack" by thousands of his followers, Bogle founded the Vanguard Group in 1974 and made it into the most respected mutual fund company in the world. At 82, he champions his pioneering efforts on behalf of low-cost index investing. After the tech bubble disaster this was a man we wanted to know more about—a lot more.

He created and introduced the first index fund, Vanguard 500 (VFINX), in 1976. He continued indexing the major asset classes discussed in chapter 4. In 1999 *Fortune Magazine* named Bogle one of the four investment giants of the twentieth century.

Bogle's adversaries are the same as ours—those employed in the financial industry who put their interests over us. That did it: we found a like-minded professional friend. His investment strategy isn't beholden to Wall Street's values of charging enormous costs and encouraging reckless trading. His reasonable philosophy of investing fits our non-competitive California hippie values. Bogle's indexing strategy rarely trades. It provides average market returns. A good investment benefits all parties involved. Nothing cutthroat—it's straight forward and ethical.

We were relieved to find a common sense approach that built on what was congruent with our comfort level and values. Legions of investors have been attracted to indexing for their core holdings. Vanguard has $1.7 trillion in assets held for millions of people, making it the largest mutual fund company in the world.

Bogle's personal ethics pervade Vanguard's corporate culture differentiating it from other investment companies. Vanguard has no shareholders. It isn't publicly traded or privately owned, unlike almost all the other Wall Street investment firms. The investors own Vanguard--people like us who buy its index fund shares. Vanguard has one master—the clients.

The Vanguard executives embrace genuine fiduciary responsibility to their clients as evidenced by the following three basic Vanguard principles (Vanguard.com website):

1. *We're owned by the funds that are owned by clients like you, so we have no competing loyalties. We don't pay profits to a private owner or stockholders. We always keep your long-term interests in mind—even closing funds when necessary to keep away short-term performance chasers.*

2. *Your funds are at-cost. You pay what it costs us to run the funds. By investing at cost, you keep more of your returns working for you, giving you a great start on reaching your financial goals.*

3. We help you focus on the long term. We don't get caught up in the emotion of Wall Street's mood swings—and we tell you why you shouldn't either. We follow a disciplined long-term approach through good markets and bad. That's just another way we keep your interests first.

Their [Wall Street] self-interest will not soon change. But as an investor, you must look after your self-interest.

—John Bogle

Vanguard's employee bonuses are only approved for cost-saving ideas: those which benefit their clients. Can you imagine Goldman Sachs approving their millions upon millions in employee bonuses due to cost saving ideas which directly benefit their clients? Not a chance, that will *never* happen. Vanguard and Wall Street's corporate cultures are as disparate as Ghandi and Madoff.

Indexing and the Active/Passive Debate

Indexing is often called passive investing. Indexing refers to the types of stocks in a basket, an asset class, e.g., the S&P 500 (discussed in the last chapter). The investor is passive and patient in the sense scrutiny is simplified. It doesn't require close analysis by the investor or a manager. The S&P 500 index replicates and follows Wall Street's S&P 500 asset class.

Passive investors purchase indexes with the intention of long-term appreciation with limited buying and selling. The old joke is passive portfolio owners do not merit bragging rights at parties. Passive portfolios by definition may not shine in the short term. Over long periods of time indexes beat managed funds 70% to 80% due to low costs and reduced trading expenses (see references).

Actively Managed Investors Fight Back

If you doubt the tenacity of active managed investors' extreme grip on bragging rights, we offer Steve's first-hand experience at an Association of Individual Investors (AAII) meeting at the Skirball Center in Los Angeles with hundreds of investors. Steve struck up a conversation with an elderly gentleman while standing in the line at the coffee break. The gentleman believed the first speaker was too "bearish" and "negative" about the future (January, 2008). Steve said, "Since nobody knows, I don't worry about the future. I have a 30 percent/70 percent stock bond split in a diversified portfolio which will take me through either bear or bull markets."

This fellow shouted back at Steve drawing attention from others in line and said, "I will never have a diversified portfolio because you will lose money in the U.S. stock market!" He cut Steve off and flung around to talk with his friend. "I invest in India," Steve heard him say to his friend. His friend said she invested in China.

Tom Petruno, former Los Angeles Times financial columnist, was the featured speaker when the meeting reconvened. He opened with the uncertainty of the markets in the months and years ahead, suggesting, "I know you heard this before and some people don't want to hear it again but the best strategy is to diversify." Steve looked around the room to see if his ex-"friend" was leaving in revulsion. Petruno made Steve's point. Diversification is a primary principle of investing. Many people don't get it.

You have been warned. This guy's reaction to Steve's comment was hilarious. It isn't easy in the day and life of a passive investor. Active management aficionados have little patience for the slow-as-you-go, non-competitive, diversified indexing strategy and they remain adamant.

Invest in the Broadest Possible Way

We love the idea of investing in the broad economies of the United States and the world. The Vanguard Total Stock Market index (VTSMX) invests in the United States domestic economy, nearly all available publicly traded companies. The Vanguard International Stock Index (VGTSX) invests in the entire planetary economy outside of the U.S., including China and India. Steve didn't have a chance to say to the elderly gentleman and his friend that he invests in India and China too.

Actively managed mutual funds invest in the manager's idea or a particular sector of the economy -- or as the gentleman at the AAII meeting proposed, India. Active investors intend to profit from short-term price fluctuations. They believe short-term investments will be profitable. That's why we shun active management -- it's not diversified in the broadest possible sense. We painfully learned this lesson from the tech crash. We thought diversification was investing in hundreds of technology companies. And those fund managers are expensive.

Active managers often claim they can beat the market benchmarks. The law of averages predicts some active fund managers will do well, sometimes for years in a row. Bill Miller is one such manager, having managed Legg Mason Capital Management fund since 1990, beating the S&P 500 until 2005. The S&P 500 index recovered the difference and then some. Since 1990 Legg Mason gained 500 percent and the S&P 500 gained 544 percent. Over time indexes will provide strong results.

Advisers don't make money selling indexed funds. Index investing doesn't require special teams of experts to select the stocks. On the other hand the suits who sell managed funds will present their angle inviting you into their special circle of customers, privileged to benefit from their analysts' special expertise. If you use their ticker symbol to compare their annual expense rate with the cost of an index you may be surprised. Index funds are about one fifth the cost of the average managed fund. If the salesperson can't provide you with a five letter 'ticker,' his or her offer is proprietary, meaning it's not available for comparison with those funds traded on the open market.

Wall Street managers and brokers charge too much. How much is too much? When you subtract the published expenses and trading costs the net return to us will be less than the average market returns. "Reversion to the mean is the dominant factor in long-term mutual fund returns," writes John Bogle.

We do not buy and sell at random. We avoid pesky little costs such as 12(b)1 marketing charges which go toward sales commissions and acquiring new customers. It may not seem like a lot but over many investing years you don't want to be paying money which should be in your pocket instead of some suit's. Aren't you paying an annual expense rate? Some people pay another one percent management fee on top, along with a 12(b)1 fee.

Our middle school math taught us the powerful benefits of compounding. Of course the lesson is to participate in compounding of assets for phenomenal gains. But few understand compounding can work against us. So why should you permit those ongoing costs to compound for the benefit of Wall Street instead of you the investor?

Have you heard about revenue sharing? These are kickback fees paid out of annual expenses to co-managers in some retirement plans. The sales force doesn't call them kickbacks, but that's what they seem like when these fees are not disclosed. This is a lack of transparency. Enter the ticker symbol on a financial site and check out the charges: front-end loads, back-end loads, 12(b)1 fees, revenue sharing and broker fees which accrue with frequent turnover. Revenue sharing is hidden.

The turnover percent refers to the amount of buying and selling during one year. One of our many tech funds,

Fidelity Select Electronics, returned over a 100 percent in 1999 with a turnover rate of 166 percent. Thankfully we are out of those high turnover funds because they lost their fantastic gains. Frequent trades are a loser's game. Fidelity Electronics returned 100 percent but we never captured those gains because the fund lost its value faster than a new car when driven off the dealer's lot. We have subsequently learned the higher the turnover rate the greater amount you are paying in trading costs. "For investors as a whole, returns decrease as motion increases" (Bogle, *Little Book of Common Sense Investing*).

A word about Exchange Traded Funds (ETFs). These funds have three-letter tickers and can be traded in the market in a moment's notice: ideal for hedge funds and day traders with hidden benefits for long-term investors. First, ETFs draw active traders away from the long-term investments we use; they want fast action in the market. We are after steady gains rather than opportunistic quick profits (or losses). Second, their frequent trading increases their expenses. According to Richard Ferri, this keeps our traditional mutual fund costs lower—good news for us. The flies are eating the...while we grow the roses. In 2004 ETFs were new products. We were spared the temptation.

Excessive Trading

The financial media blames individual investors for excessive trades. But the solid contrary evidence shows it's the professionals who frequently trade. "Professional investors as a whole are responsible for about 90 percent of all stock market trading," according to Ellis and Malkiel's, *The Elements of Investing*. Peter Lynch wrote 25 years ago in his book, "Beating the Street" "the vast majority of Magellan investors stayed put and did nothing. They saw the Great Correction [1987 crash] for what it was, and not as the beginning of the end of civilization."

How much does the industry trade? By far the largest action of the stock market and the people in the business is to *trade*. Up to billions of shares are traded each day. Why? Former Secretary of the Security & Exchange Commission (SEC), Arthur Levitt explains in great detail in his book, *Take on the Street*, how Wall Street insiders use trades to make money. Most of the trading activity is not in our best interest. And Mr. Levitt knows as he tried to make those trades transparent when he was the Secretary of the SEC. The industry fought him all the way.

You know Wall Street bonuses are sucked out of every loophole or derivative they can create. In this corporate republic, the well-bought Congress won't increase funding for SEC auditors. Political candidates and many legislatures blame regulators for our national financial ills. The dismantling of appropriate regulations began under President Clinton. This may take us to ruin. The point is not to depend on regulations to help us.

Kathy Kristof, columnist for *Kiplinger's* Personal Finance and *CBS MoneyWatch*, would agree it's the professionals who trade at every opportunity. She wrote in her book, *Investing 101,* that during the Asian currency crises in 1997, the Dow Jones Industrial average dropped 300 points in one day. She talked to financial professionals and individual investors to find out what was going on. She wrote: "Given the fast-paced trading and the rapid decline in stock prices, it was clear *somebody* was panicking." It was the professionals who were acting like amateurs. She wrote, "beads of sweat were forming under their starched white collars and gray pinstriped suits." When she called dozens of everyday investors, "A few were at home. A few were at work. Some were at the baseball game. They were not breathless. They were not sweating." No-one called their brokers to sell. Kristof's anecdotal one day observation should not be trivialized. We don't need to sweat either.

The financial industry loves volatility: making money when the market goes up or down. It doesn't matter to them. Every time someone sells, another buys, both think they're smart. It's always the brokers who profit from the transaction. These people claim they add value for customers—*pure nonsense.* The financial media reports investors should buy this stock or fund because of good news or bad news here or abroad with this or that industry. The cultural narrative encourages and rewards trading. Buying and selling generates commissions and bonuses. This level of activity is known as "churning." Stock brokers and financial advisers get to enjoy the sweet butter it produces, not us.

What does this mean for us? Financial education will improve our chances of protecting ourselves more than regulations or deregulations. Invest in all available companies and the world-wide economies *not* the financial establishment recommendations. We trade to maintain balance in our portfolio, once or twice a year.

Your Financial Adviser

Only a suspicious person (not us, of course) would suggest a broker who has your signature and your approval to trade on your behalf might churn your investments for their new Mercedes or an elite private school tuition payment to compensate for a slow business month. Unsuspecting investors pay transaction costs for this adviser initiated transaction: legal, frequent and unethical.

Commission-based advisers rarely use Vanguard or TIAA-CREF (TIAA-CREF will be discussed shortly). Vanguard's protections against frequent trading are designed to keep the opportunists at bay in favor of long term investors. Neither company pays commissions. Because there are no commissions it's as unlikely as man-bites-dog news that any agent, adviser or broker will recommend either of these companies. (Chapter 11 focuses on locating a fee-only financial adviser who would be more than happy to recommend low cost options.)

Speculation and Risk

Webster defines speculation "an assumption of _unusual_ business risk in hopes of obtaining commensurate gains." All of the unusual business risk you want can be found in hedge funds, derivatives, options, futures, margin trading, short-selling and numerous other speculative undertakings. We avoid these alternative ventures because our financial goal achieves average gains by investing in the broadest markets possible.

The tech and real estate bubbles gained momentum as hundreds of thousands of investors took unusual risks. It doesn't help that others were just as unknowing. We mentioned our factoring escapade which lost us $5,000. Not so bad considering we lost a million later, but still…

What is _usual_ risk? We don't have to win with each of our indexed mutual funds. While all market investing involves risk, over time the market goes up. Sometimes bonds lead but more often it's stocks: domestic or foreign. John Bogle recommends: "Own them all." He points out the futility of searching for the one company to invest in or a five-star rated mutual fund recommended by your broker.

Armed with this new information and a solid rationale of risk and return, we were ready to pay off our mortgage and make our basic portfolio moves.

Our Transition

In January 2004, fortified with an improved portfolio (Table 10, page 81), we jumped at the chance to pay off our house. We sold Microsoft, Intel, and Cisco Systems and gave ourselves a mortgage burning party. It was a relief to clean house and start over debt free, allowing

Dan to reposition his holdings and Steve to increase both 403(b) and Roth contributions.

We transferred the tech sector funds and tech stocks into lower costing diversified funds. Dan liked the Dodge and Cox fund family (U.S. Large Cap DODGX, International DODFX, and Balanced DODBX), Loomis Sayles' corporate bonds (LSBDX) and Vanguard's Intermediate Investment Grade Bonds (VFICX). Some of the proceeds went to the Vanguard Small Cap (NAESX) and Emerging Markets (VEIEX) funds. He had both managed and indexed funds.

Steve's Transition to TIAA CREF and Vanguard

Steve transferred his IRA tech funds from INVESCO and Fidelity to Vanguard. He stopped putting new money into INVESCO because there was a lower cost option for his 403(b) at LAUSD: TIAA-CREF (TC). This is an acronym for Teachers Insurance Annuity Association – College Retirement Equities Fund. Steve invested new money in TC's Equity Index (Total Stock Market Index equivalent), Global Equity and a Bond Market Fund.

TC remains *the* retirement institution for higher education and many non-profit organizations since its inception in 1918. TC's mission statement says it all. From their website: tiaa-cref.org:

Serving the Greater Good

For over 90 years, TIAA-CREF has been helping those in the academic, medical, cultural and research fields plan for and live in retirement...In keeping with our *strong <u>nonprofit heritage</u>, we offer <u>low fees</u>, a <u>long-term</u> <u>approach to investing</u>...products and services provided by <u>consultants who never receive commissions</u>. Instead, they are <u>compensated primarily on how well they serve you</u>, <u>not what they sell you</u>.* (Edited for space and underlined for emphasis).

Steve was excited to discover TC has a similar corporate culture as Vanguard, reflected in their mission statement. After ten years of advocacy, a quality 403(b) company became available from his employer, LAUSD.

Steve's knowledge of the big picture philosophies of Vanguard and TC led his decision to shun actively managed funds. He invested all new money into index funds and bonds in these two great companies.

He thought Dan would do the same, but Dan opted for about half his holdings in indexed and the rest in actively managed funds. This led to some debate at home. Despite our agreement to own low cost investments and avoid individual stocks, Dan stuck with his trio of Dodge and Cox funds and Loomis Sayles. Steve was okay with Dan's active management leanings as long they were low cost. Besides, Dan had some of his 403(b) money in Vanguard indexes as well and recall a decade ago Dan recommended Vanguard Wellington for Steve's 403(b). Steve has the first claim to being the indexer in our family.

Advice from a Fee-Only Fiduciary

We found a great advisor, Scott Dauenhauer, Certified Financial Professional (CFP), who helped merge our existing portfolio with indexed funds in 2005.

Scotty dropped by on one of Steve's 403(b) informational investment group meetings Steve co-founded to help teacher colleagues at LAUSD. Professionals would sometimes visit. Scotty was a wholly different professional. His philosophy mirrored Vanguard and TC corporate ethical fibers. He was a 27-year-old straight shooter with keen intelligence who agreed that teachers were getting taken by annuity rip-offs. Most important he respected and thought, as Steve did, Vanguard and TC are high-quality companies—Steve was sold on the spot. Only a handful of professionals see what we see in Vanguard and TC.

The horde of 403(b) agents and most financial advisers despise TC. How do we know? Ask your adviser. This is a simple way to find out if the person handling your money has your best interests. Scotty passed Steve's "test" question with an "AAA" rating. He is as rare as an albino dolphin in a sea of "sharks."

We asked him to look at our holdings as we were transitioning to the major asset classes and index funds and paid his hourly fee. A fiduciary advisor assists with developing a plan. Fiduciaries don't earn additional money from the plan, including commissions. Genuine fiduciaries don't recommend funds which give any part of your investment back to themselves without your knowledge. Just as important, any recommendations are geared to fit the client's overall plan.

Scotty included our favorite funds accommodating

Dan's aggressive investing and suggested some additional assets (Table 9). He helped us visualize the goal of a diversified portfolio including the major asset classes as reflected by the indexing strategy.

It is difficult to get a man to understand something when his salary depends upon his not understanding it.

—**Upton Sinclair**

Table 9
Portfolio Recommended by Scott Dauenhauer, CFP

Asset Class	Stock	$700,000 Allocation	Mutual Fund
Large-Cap	21 %	14.7 %	$102,900 Vanguard TSM
Large-Value	29 %	20.3 %	$142,100 Dodge/Cox Stk
Mid-Cap	5 %	3.5 %	$24,500 Vanguard Mid-cap index
Small-Cap Value	5 %	3.5 %	$24,500 Vanguard Small-cap value
Small-Cap	5 %	3.5%	$24,500 Vanguard small-cap index
Real Estate	5%	3.5%	$24,500 Vanguard REITS
International Value	25%	15%	$122,500 Dodge/Cox International
Emerging Markets	5%	3.5%	$24,500 Vanguard Emerg Mtk.
	Bonds		
Fixed	66%	20%	$140,000 TIAA Traditional
Fixed	24%	10%	$70,000 Vanguard Inflation Protect.
Equity/Bond Split	70%/30%		

It was what we wanted, except the Equity/Bond Split of 70% stock/30% bond is appropriate for a 30 year-old investor, not a couple approaching full retirement. A general rule is to allocate a percentage of bonds which match your age. For example, if you are 33 years old, allocate about 30-35 percent in bonds, with the rest 70-75 percent in stocks.

Steve found an age-appropriate allocation on the Vanguard website which offers a 30 percent/70 percent risk and return balance, an ideal portfolio for us (Table 10). The average annual return of 7.3% would be our retirement benchmark for our revised portfolio

(See the Appendix A for additional Vanguard portfolio allocation models).

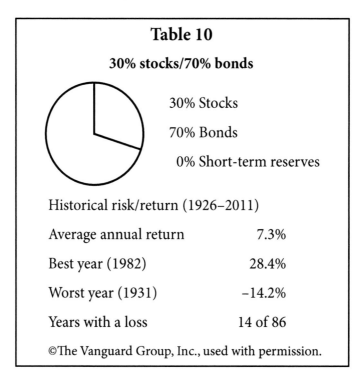

Table 10

30% stocks/70% bonds

30% Stocks

70% Bonds

0% Short-term reserves

Historical risk/return (1926–2011)

Average annual return	7.3%
Best year (1982)	28.4%
Worst year (1931)	−14.2%
Years with a loss	14 of 86

©The Vanguard Group, Inc., used with permission.

The Vanguard Model Portfolio was a revelation to Steve, but Dan wasn't on board. He balked at the 7.3% return. He didn't sell his actively managed Dodge & Cox funds. The funds did well for a few years until he read a report in 2007 which led to his metamorphosis.

Like Father, Unlike Son

Dan's next experience was pivotal. He had been adamant about keeping his managed funds. He changed his mind due to a curious series of events. His conversion came as he cared for his terminally ill father.

Ninety year-old Harry was dying but eager to discuss investing. A perennial day-trading speculator, he bought individual stocks requiring a gimmick: a new fangled medical device, a gaudy construction technique or based on some cockamamie recommendation from one of the numerous investment newsletters he read. He called Ameritrade several times a day to check the volume and the price of his last favorite stock: Taser (TASR).

Several newsletters guided his investment decisions. Many of the articles made buy and sell recommendation with tales of riches or doom to bolster their touts. One article stood out. Dan saw a list of banks and brokerage firms over-leveraged in risky questionable mortgage-backed securities, derivatives and credit default swaps. Nobody in the news media was interested in this story yet—few people understood these instruments. The list in the newsletter included Citibank, Bank of America, Lehman Brothers, AIG, Goldman Sachs, Morgan Stanley, Bear Stearns and many other subsequent "bail-out-ees."

Dan wasn't taken by conspiracy theories. He made money from his mutual funds. Steve nagged him about his risky allocation in actively managed funds and dismissed anything from a newsletter. In addition to the active management philosophical argument which got nowhere, Steve reminded him his equity exposure was appropriate for a 30-year-old but not a 65-year-old retiree. Steve recognized Dan's actively managed funds were doing well in the bull market and so were Steve's indexes.

Steve was concerned Dan would lose his gains because of excessive risk, a repeat of the tech bubble. We both recognized the country and the stock market were in another bubble, the real estate bubble. Dan wasn't convinced about reducing his 65% aggressive equity exposure.

As time passed and Dan's portfolio grew, Steve's anxiety about Dan's aggressive strategy grew too. Dan remained excited and Steve remembered "excitement" wasn't a friend. It was a warning about taking too much risk which turned out to be a disaster in the last bubble. In desperation Steve said, "If you lose money again I'm not going to retire. I'll need to work to build my pension and add to my 403(b) to make up your losses." It wasn't a threat (well, perhaps a little). Steve had the advantage as Dan wanted him to retire. During the summer of 2007, a break in our standoff ensued.

Bear Stearns

Dan took serious notice during August 2007 when Bear Stearns attracted major headlines. It was one of the at-risk financial firms reported in his father's newsletter. When CNBC's Jim Cramer dismissed the idea Bear Stearns might be in trouble, Dan knew otherwise. He remembered the prescient newsletter. It was like a tremor warning of an earthquake. In March, 2008 Cramer defended Bear Stearns *again*, saying it would not go bankrupt: a bad call. The one thing we agreed on–*never* listen to Jim Cramer.

Dan looked up his fund holdings in Yahoo. There's

lots of information including the percent of money in various market sectors. His best performing managed funds were overloaded with those financial firms on the list. Oh Lordy, did Dan start to move. He transferred his share of the portfolio from active managed equity funds into indexed fixed accounts: income funds, corporate bonds, investment grade bond funds and TIPS with a vengeance.

Steve was pleased *and* relieved. Fiduciaries don't recommend timing your portfolio according to what somebody writes in a newsletter. This time it was fortunate the combination of Dan's age, the newsletter and Steve's nagging caused him to change to a less risky allocation. Steve didn't care how and where Dan got his information. As long as Dan reduced his equity risk to an age appropriate allocation between stocks and bonds, Steve was satisfied. Dan was convinced the financial markets would compromise the entire stock market performance because of risky derivatives and leveraged instruments.

We were lucky he did this before the 2008 stock market crash. Still, luck is not an investment strategy nor part of a plan. Dan had always been excited by the gains in his active managed funds. This was up until mid-2007. His dad's newsletter was prophetic and scary as the mortgage market started to dissolve, followed by the rest of the stock market. By the beginning of 2008 Dan was out of his managed funds and into bonds and income funds as fast as a desert hare. He even beat the

Lehman Brothers default.

Steve retired as planned in 2008. We were on the same page. The Vanguard portfolio allocation model of a 30/70 stock bond split allocation plan has as little risk to principal as possible while achieving a reasonable retirement goal. Dan was satisfied we had enough money to retire so he accepted the 30/70 split based on the 80-year historical return of 7.3 percent.

Figure 1 shows our revised allocation after we changed from our tech heavy holdings to a significant bond allocation by January 2008. The equities were mostly in index funds, the cash in TC Traditional Annuity with diversified holdings of bonds: GNMAs, Treasuries, Corporate and TIPS. This transition started in 2004 and completed in early 2008.

We sought the middle ground and thankfully, found it. We *experienced* real market risk, acknowledged our restricted time horizon and continue to learn about stock market performance and history. With both of us retired and the real estate bubble about to burst, our new asset allocation would face its first *huge* test.

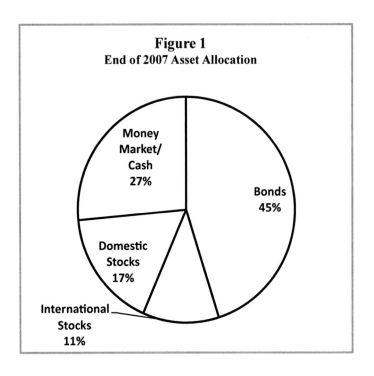

Figure 1
End of 2007 Asset Allocation

Steve Schullo and Dan Robertson

CHAPTER 6

The Big Test

(2 0 0 8)

The year began with the housing market and Dow Jones Industrial Average torn between denial and feigned exuberance. The housing bubble peaked in 2006 and began its gradual decline. The Dow hit its high in October 2007 and lost 15 percent by January 2008. The housing and stock markets were shaky, the worst since 2002.

Steve planned to retire at the end of the school year – July 1, six months hence. He was so excited he proposed, "Why not get out of L.A. where we can start anew?" Dan agreed. We picked Coachella Valley, two hours east of Los Angeles, the home of Palm Springs and several other desert resort cities, but a million miles away from the hectic big city.

We had a lot to do. The unsure fog of property value declines gave urgency to the next decisions. Home prices were declining. We were eager to get into action to sell our real estate. How would we manage the financial aspects of continually lowered home prices as we sold our home in L.A., sold our vacation condo in Palm Springs and bought a retirement home in the desert?

We had to sell the L.A. house first. We paid more than we could afford in 1981, renting the basement unit and living upstairs unfurnished until our incomes increased. Our mid-century moderne was a peaceful home on Mt. Washington near Dodger Stadium keeping us happy and busy for 27 years.

That dreaded word: Commissions

We interviewed three real estate agents to see who might handle the sale. We figured they could lower the usual six percent commission due to the slipping housing market. They gave staging tips for the interior of the house but *none* negotiated on their commissions. Furthermore, they wanted us to be ready to accept a lower selling price. The commissions *and* lowered expectations of our house price motivated us to sell the house ourselves.

Selling a house on our own was a leap of faith for two novices. We figured we'd put our "For Sale by Owner" sign next to the other open house notices at our busy neighborhood intersection and maybe get a buyer. According to real estate surveys it's neighbors or friends of neighbors who buy your house. We were no exception. Our neighbors toured the first day and we accepted their offer.

With escrow scheduled to close in May our hearts speeded. We still had a condo to sell and a home to buy. Dan found a fair price for comparable units and mailed a "For Sale" sign requesting the snowbird renters of our Palm Springs condo to tape it in the window. Two days later we got our asking price.

Both places sold right away; now we had two escrows closing in May. By selling the homes ourselves we saved about $70,000 in commissions.

Meanwhile, Dan surfed the net for homes. We had a great agent who helped us focus our search. Our choice–a home once owned by Academy Award winner Jane Wyman—located in Rancho Mirage. We moved for the first time in 27 years. We put in tile and carpets, painted, gussied up the little yard and pool, installed solar electric panels and later put in a new kitchen.

Decision Time: July 2008

This transition to our retirement home happened without portfolio worries. Still, the stock market and the housing market remained in doubt. For Steve it was quite a time to retire—three months before the greatest financial crisis since the Depression. In the summer of 2008 we had a big decision—how to diversify our real estate proceeds.

We had $400,000 of new money to infuse in our current portfolio. We asked Vanguard to help us with this important decision. We were entitled to one pro bono consult by phone.

We put the money into our three existing core

funds: the Total Bond Market Index (VBTLX –- 50 percent), Total International Market Index (VTIAX – 20 percent), and the Total Stock Market Index (VTSAX-30 percent). Because of our existing plan it was a simple decision.

Bear Sterns Lives in Dan's Head

Dan was averse to putting 50 percent of this new money into equity index funds! How ironic—after his risky active managed funds he loved before, he had become a tad tepid. This time Steve was the aggressive investor. The adviser helped by providing an objective view. We knew enough about our existing portfolio to curtail excessive risk. Steve hadn't changed his investment behavior. He was comfortable with the decision as he was looking at our entire portfolio. The inclusion of this new money fit our 30 percent/70 percent stock/bond split.

The source of Dan's reluctance was the downfall of Bear Stearns: that newsletter article *still* haunted him. Had he glimpsed a harbinger? Where to put money with these doubts? Market troubles did escalate in a few months -- would our allocation hold up?

By the middle of September 2008 we needed a vacation from the three escrows, moving and construction in our new place. "What an exciting year," we thought. We were relieved we sold both properties within weeks and we got good prices. We were also excited about our retirement home purchase and the lower price we negotiated.

Major life transitions are stressful. The Grand Canyon beckoned and we looked forward to camping on the South Rim with our Great Outdoors hiking club friends.

We felt secure our decisions tracked what we had learned from our mistakes. Our financial reincarnation was real. It's nice not to worry when you're away. We fired up the Ford 250 and pulled our Alpenlite RV/fifth wheel and ourselves to this natural wonder. Little did we know our financial discoveries and decisions from 25 years of seasoned investing would be put to a huge test. The market's torment was beginning to boil.

Where Were You?

Those of us old enough to remember the JFK assassination or 9/11 will not forget our whereabouts when we learned of these horrific historic events. When the 2008 stock market began to crash we were wiling-away-the-hours reading and watching a bull elk and his harem prance through the RV Park at the South Rim.

Steve wrote in his journal: *"Dan and I had our ears to the radio all week. In short, the Dow went down 900 points and surged 900 points to come back to exactly what it was the previous Friday. The subprime loan debacle goes on and on. The latest development was 158-year-old Lehman Brothers, a global financial service firm, went belly up. Next the largest insurance company in the world, AIG, was bailed out by the feds for a 'measly' $85 billion. Lastly, along with Lehman Brothers, the nation's safest Money Market (MM) fell below $1 a share."*

This was only the second time in history a money market fund lost money, causing quite a stir among MM funds at other institutions. Just as Dan's newsletter article predicted two years previously, the financial system was coming apart. The daily volatility was unmatched by past stock market crashes.

Equity Diversification AND Bonds

During the dot-com crash of 2000-2002 an equity diversification among the customary asset classes (large-cap, mid-cap, small-cap and international), sans tech funds, held up without a bond allocation. The tech sector had the major loss of seventy percent. At that time our friend, Joe, said his portfolio hadn't lost money during the 2000-2002 crash. Steve was dumbfounded. "How was that possible?" he thought. Joe was a teacher colleague and one of the savviest investors he knew. But still…it happened because we were over-invested in the losing sector and Joe had a properly diversified equity portfolio.

The 2008 meltdown was massive, affecting the entire stock market. All equity asset classes were ripped apart no matter how cleanly they were diversified. Joe was shocked by his 25 percent loss. He fesses up in a 403bwise. com (investment discussion forum) post: "Well, the market rebalanced my portfolio for me." His stock losses automatically increased his bond holdings percentage to the 30 percent/70 percent stock/bond allocation Steve had suggested for people in his age bracket.

Of course Joe was not alone. We learned from numerous media reports in the weeks ahead many people were caught with their investment pants down. Some retired folks lost as much as 50 percent of their nest eggs. Steve remembers reading about an 82-year-old gentleman losing $1 million from his $2 million portfolio. Why? He (and many others) did not have a bond allocation which would have lowered his portfolio risk. We lost 11.9% percent: not as bad as the total stock market benchmark which lost more than 37 percent. Figure 2 shows our stock/bond split at the end of 2008.

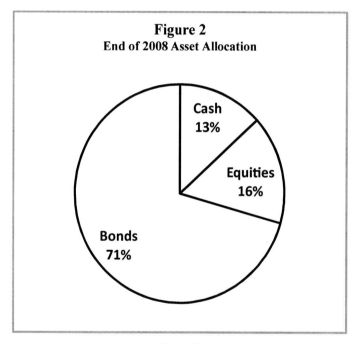

Figure 2
End of 2008 Asset Allocation

Cash 13%

Equities 16%

Bonds 71%

Trust?

National Public Radio reporters asked people for their reactions to the financial crisis and the remedies undertaken by Congress to address it. Most were angry the financial industry got bailout money in the wake of the generous deregulation legislation passed by

Congress in 1999. The industry was saved by a type of perverse reward system for their reckless behavior and without culpability: all funded by taxpayers. Their pervasive insidious greed even went untaxed.

There have been minimal consequences due to a lack of political and judicial oversight. Many home buyers remain caught in the housing bubble sinkhole erroneously betting property values could only go up, justifying those hideous loans on meager incomes (Recall the recency effect of the tech bubble). The lenders and rating agencies approved loans to unqualified people and gave AAA ratings to toxic securities.

We both felt badly for those folks caught in this economic quagmire. Quoting from Steve's journal September 19th, 2008: *"After listening to the anger expressed, we realized that we were not angry at what is happening because we have never trusted the professional financiers in the first place. Since we have already been burned, we protected ourselves by self-education and followed the wisdom, strategy and philosophy of John Bogle. He says over and over don't trust the pros without verification."* Neither should you. After getting burned by annuity agents and the tech bubble, we never trusted the big banks, investment firms or well-known brokerage houses.

When it comes to the financial industry, trust is just a buzzword. Wall Street reveals their morality in their actions that caused the crisis and reaction to the bailouts. They cost taxpayers a bundle. Have we heard a public thank you for the bailout?

Unlike the dot com crash more investors were negatively affected by this debacle. 2008 ended okay for us because we constructed a portfolio with a stock/bond split appropriate for our ages. We sat tight with the same allocation as shown in Figure 2 as we entered the New Year, 2009. The next chapter reveals the ensuing three years of portfolio performance and how it bounced back and grew.

CHAPTER 7

Aftermath—Our Phoenix

(2 0 0 9 - 2 0 1 1)

Our stock/bond split portfolio helped us escape
much of the ravaging experienced by most investors
in the 2008 crash. This chapter shows how our asset
allocation performed in the immediate aftermath. It's
one thing to escape crashes but quite another to grow as
the broader stock market struggles to recover. We detail
a three-year case-study you may find useful for your
portfolio construction and management.

We were both retired. We took regular distributions
from our nest egg for the first time. Even with predictable
volatility and uncertainty over the last three years—2009-
2011--the 2008 crash turned out not so bad. For many
investors it was disastrous if they were overloaded with
individual stocks or stock funds. It's dreadful for those
approaching retirement who were still on the financial
roller-coaster and took risks they didn't understand.

Dan retired in 2000 when he turned 59. Steve was the primary wage provider for three years until Dan began taking his social security. Steve was thrilled to support Dan's early retirement. Recall Dan supported Steve's bid to return to college decades before. When Steve retired in 2008 at 61, eight years after Dan, we were debt free and started a new life in the desert southwest.

The volatile market continued at the beginning of 2009 and reemerged in late summer, 2011. This latest volatility had to do with the financial fallout which started in the United States in 2008 and spread to Europe. The continent struggles with its debt while our own national debt and political intransigence for finding solutions ensures more insecurity. As investors we live with uncertainty in all of its forms and adapt.

Distributions

To assure your portfolio lasts the rest of your life the general rule of thumb limits annual distributions to 4 percent of principle or less. We were fortunate we limited our distributions to less than 4 percent due to Steve's pension and Dan's Social Security. Changing from the accumulation to the distribution stage demands an attitude shift. Starting this at the beginning of a national maelstrom created a nervous excitement. We wondered how the retirement portfolio would perform without adding new money. After years of accumulating we knew how portfolios increase and fall along with blood pressure. But what will it be like taking money out in the wake of the recent crash?

We waited until our portfolio regained some of its losses from 2008 before taking money out a little at a time. As it turned out, 2009 was an excellent year for the stock market and our portfolio. It returned 13.9 percent (see Table 11). We cautiously withdrew money to fund the new kitchen. Despite the distributions in these three years our portfolio gained back the 11.9 percent loss suffered in 2008 (+$179,209). The portfolio replenished itself, thanks to the last three years of a bull market.

Table 11 shows the growth over three years. We withdrew a total of $136,449 while our portfolio grew a net of $230,339 (after distributions were subtracted from gross portfolio growth total in Table 11). That's the sweet spot of retiring, using money from the nest egg while the portfolio grows more than taken out. After three years we gained confidence in our distribution plan.

Table 11 2009-2011 Portfolio				
Year	Distribution	Gross Portfolio Growth*	Value of Portfolio	Returns
End of 2009	$52,500	$179,209	$1,410,695	13.9%
End of 2010	$44,773	$149,538	$1,515,460	10.6%
End of 2011	$39,176	$38,031	$1,514,315	2.5%
3-Year Totals	$136,449	$366,778		

*Distributions were left in to calculate the returns. For example, for 2009 return, we divided the gross growth of $179,209/$1,283,986=13.9% return for 2009. The $1,283,986 is the value of portfolio on December 31, 2008.

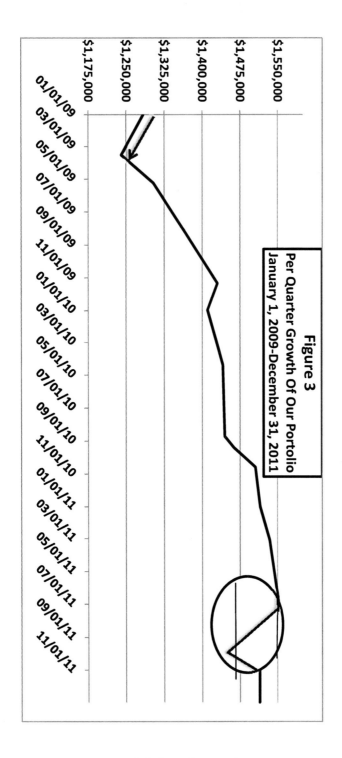

Figure 3
Per Quarter Growth Of Our Portolio
January 1, 2009-December 31, 2011

Steve Schullo and Dan Robertson

Figure 3 shows the value of our portfolio over three years. It wasn't smooth sailing. No equity and bond portfolio exposed to market risk is immune from fluctuation. In the first 3 months of 2009, it continued to lose value from 2008 (as illustrated by the arrow). Suddenly without warning the markets changed course starting a bull market on March 6, 2009. The upward trend continued until August 7, 2011. The stock market began a major double-digit decline lasting for two months (refer to the circle in Figure 3). The only other crash on May 6, 2010—dubbed the "Flash Crash", had no material effect on stocks as it recovered within the same trading day. Continuing fears and rabid bickering in Congress with the word, *compromise*, gone forever were primary reasons reported for the market decline in 2011. Plus the down-grading of treasuries and the threatening European bankruptcies added to the crisis.

We didn't care about the constant serial chatter. These stories were real, of course. They increased our resolve to stick to our plan and go about our business of completing our latest projects—installing a huge dining room window and planning a trip to Africa with Dan's sister Cathy and her husband Glenn. There will always be uncertainty with associated financial drama.

Media pundits will use any economic certainty or uncertainty to convince investors to buy, sell or trade something. It's their business and their right to sell news. We *ignore all of it*, have a financial plan and buy or sell within the parameters of rebalancing. We go by the assumption of 100 percent uncertainty now and in the future. To wish for certain and safe periods to invest is futile, like expecting a broker to recommend Vanguard or TIAA CREF.

Many people don't get it and fall for the trivial noise. One of our friends told us he sold his stocks and put it into cash in August, 2011. We were surprised, but upon closer examination, he did what he believed was in his best interest—he wanted to stop the bleeding. Was this a smart move? Let's look at this from a long-term view. By the end of 2011 the broader market averages rebounded (after the circle in Figure 3) ending the year where it started (Detailed look at each year will be presented).

At this writing in September 2012, our portfolio has surpassed the July, 2011 highs by a healthy 8 percent YTD. We don't know what our friend did since he sold his equity position. He likely missed out on the rebound and will get back in after it's too late. Isn't getting back in the market *always* a problem? If our friend had seen this bigger picture fourteen months later, do you think he would have bailed? Of course not. And neither would you. He over reacted to the plethora of financial news which spreads fear and causes the market to decline short-term. Investors who sell in a panic don't have a long-term plan or take on too much risk.

Table 12 illustrates the returns of most of the funds we own compared to the market averages (space limitations restrict listing all holdings). We think that it's instructive to show how our portfolio performed compared to the stock and bond market averages. We combined these data in a single table for easy comparisons across the 3-3/4 years and across asset classes. Notice that some of our funds revealed volatility.

Table 12			
Our Portfolio Stock and Bond Mutual Fund Returns Compared to Broad Market Averages in **bold**			
Our *Bond* Fund Total Returns			
Bond Funds	2009	2010	2011	2012—3Q YTD
Vanguard Total Bond Market Index	6.0 percent	6.5 percent	7.7 percent	3.96 percent
Vanguard TIPS	10.8 percent	6.2 percent	13.3 percent	7.2 percent
Vanguard GNMA	5.3 percent	6.9 percent	7.8 percent	2.5 percent
Vanguard Intermediate Treasuries	-1.7 percent	7.4 percent	9.9 percent	2.8 percent
Vanguard Investment Grade (Corp. Bonds)	1.4 percent	10.6 percent	7.6 percent	8.4 percent
Loomis Sayles Bond	37.2 percent*	13.6 percent	3.8 percent	12.2 percent
Barclays U.S. Aggregate Bond Index	**5.9 percent**	**6.5 percent**	**7.8 percent**	**4.0 percent**
Our *Stock* Index Fund Total Returns			
Equity Funds	2009	2010	2011	2012—3Q YTD
Vanguard Total Stock Market Index	28.7 percent	17.4 percent	.9 percent	17.8 percent
Vanguard Total International Stock Index	36.7 percent	11.1 percent	-14.5 percent	12.4 percent
Vanguard Extended Market Index	37.4 percent	27.4 percent	-3.6 percent	16.1 percent
Dow Jones Industrial Ave.	**18.8 percent**	**11.02 percent**	**5.6 percent**	**12.2 percent**
S&P 500	**26.5 percent**	**12.8 percent**	**Unchanged**	**16.4 percent**
Nasdaq	**43.9 percent**	**16.9 percent**	**-1.8 percent**	**20.7 percent**
Overall Portfolio* Returns*			
Year	2009	2010	2011	2012—3Q YTD
Our Portfolio Return	13.96 percent	10.6 percent	2.5 percent	8.0 percent

*The Loomis Sayles stellar 2009 return was a rebound from a massive loss, a -22.1 percent 2008 return, its only loss since its 1991 inception.

**These returns are what we actually received as opposed to the performance of each fund. The returns are calculated before subtracting distributions (Table 11).

One market average needs an introduction—Barclays Aggregate Bond Index. It's a standard for comparing the performance of bond holdings. Often used by professionals, Barclays' broad based bond index, maintained by Barclays Capital represents investment grade bonds (aka corporate bonds), treasury securities, government agency and mortgage-backed bonds. We chose this benchmark to compare our individual bond funds because it represents intermediate-term bonds which match the primary maturity date of our bonds. With the exception of TIPS, our bond funds can be compared to this index. It provides a ballpark idea of how our individual bond funds performed.

2009

Our Portfolio Fights Back
from the Mighty Fracas of 2008

Figure 4 shows the portfolio return and volatility over the course of 2009. The leading news for the New Year was the March 6, 2009 low—DJIA tanked to 6443 and the S&P 500 hovered at 666, 12-year lows. Unbelievably the market retreated all the way back to 1997 levels. The bottom made major media headlines for weeks. The pundits predicted gloom and doom, "the markets will not recover for years," blah, blah, blah. Our portfolio followed suit like a private marching to the sergeant's orders, also losing value. We were fortunate we still remembered the lesson learned from the 2000-2002 crash. We held *firm* as the mess of 2008 lingered. Our portfolio lost 3.4 percent in the first three months.

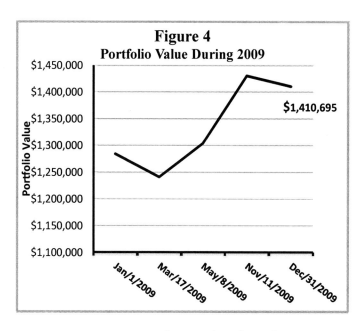

Figure 4
Portfolio Value During 2009

$1,410,695

Was 2009 going to be another horrific year? No. Once again the media "noisters" were wrong. The market digested the repercussions in the aftermath of the financial crisis, real estate crash, federal bailouts and the ensuing recession with unemployment rising every month coupled with a new presidency. Markets don't like change and uncertainty—and there was plenty of both during the first quarter. We don't mean to trivialize doubt, but as investors it's easier to practice diligence and patience with a plan than without. These powerful traits aren't discussed when instant gratification is the norm.

Have we collectively forgotten the opposite of instant gratification? LAUSD famed teacher Rafe Esquith created an economic program for six graders and wrote this observation in his book, *There Are No Shortcuts:* "Some children spend all their money...others

never buy until the end of the year because I reserve…
the coolest items. In this way, students learn about
saving, planning, and the most important concept of
all, delayed gratification."

It wasn't long ago a cross-country journey might
take days or weeks. Today some of us complain, "My
flight was delayed 20 minutes" forgetting how fortunate
we are to have greater conveniences than our parents
and grandparents. Even twittering isn't fast enough for
some in spite of the communication revolution. We
default to impatience, particularly when the market is
uncertain and painfully slow. Uncertainty has one
redeeming and little known value—it's an uncontrollable
constant. It's always around like the annuity sales force
at your place of business. Buck-up and deal with it.

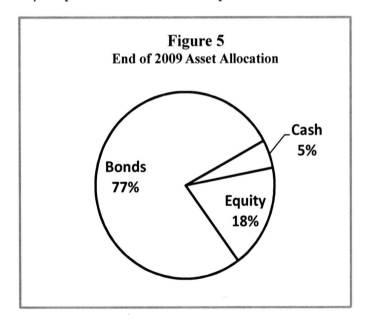

Figure 5
End of 2009 Asset Allocation

Cash
5%

Bonds
77%

Equity
18%

Figure 5 illustrates our asset allocation at the end of 2009. We rebalanced our 13 percent cash holdings into equities and bonds. We sold some of our bond allocation to purchase equities, but bonds kept increasing in value too. In 2009, our bonds increased about 10 percent in value and our equities gained 22 percent. We were still out of balance with 18 percent equities and overweight in bonds, 77 percent. The great news for 2009—the market recovered from March through the rest of the year. Our portfolio followed along as expected by returning 13.9 percent.

2010 Portfolio Performance

2010 was another excellent year. Although the broad stock market returns were lower in 2010 than 2009, Barclay's bond index was higher returning 6.5 percent in 2010. Our portfolio returned 10.6 percent (Table 11), thanks to bonds. We are not complaining about a $104,765 net gain after using some of the distributions to fund the construction of that new kitchen.

Figure 6 shows the portfolio coming back to our original 30 percent/70 percent equity bond split. We use the money market account for the cash portion to rebalance our portfolio or spend. We take regular distributions from the interest earned from two bond bonds, keeping well below the 4 percent limit. Dan takes a monthly distribution from Loomis Sayles and Steve takes a distribution from the Vanguard Total Bond Market.

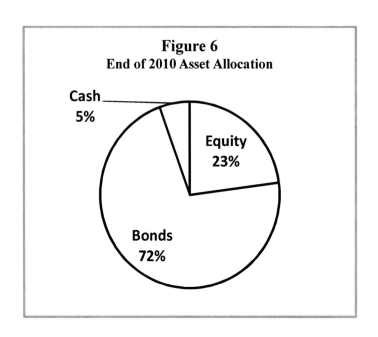

Figure 6
End of 2010 Asset Allocation

Cash 5%

Equity 23%

Bonds 72%

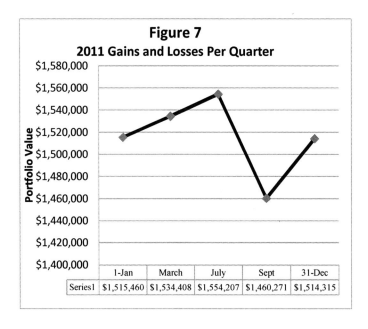

Figure 7
2011 Gains and Losses Per Quarter

	1-Jan	March	July	Sept	31-Dec
Series1	$1,515,460	$1,534,408	$1,554,207	$1,460,271	$1,514,315

Portfolio Value

The Stock Market Pulls Back

After two and a half years of solid, upward growth,

the market took a 20 percent haircut during August and September, 2011. Figure 7 illustrates how our portfolio gained from the beginning of the year to July. Then the market declined. Our portfolio declined almost $100,000 in value before creeping back to the same level at the beginning of the year and regaining that "loss."

Double digit returns for 2009-2010 didn't last for long. We managed a 2.5 percent return because of our bond allocation. The international stocks dragged our portfolio down. International funds lost 14.5 percent while the Barclay's bond index soared to 7.8 percent. The bonds pulled our portfolio out of a certain loss for the year.

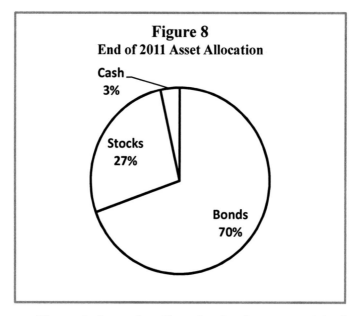

Figure 8
End of 2011 Asset Allocation

Cash 3%

Stocks 27%

Bonds 70%

Figure 8 shows the allocation back to our original stock/bond split. All of our bonds are up for the third year in a row. During the August/September downturn we took the opportunity to sell some bonds and purchase stocks. Stock funds were priced low so we added our newest investment: Vanguard Wellesley (VWIAX). It's a balanced fund providing *both* bond interest and stock dividend payments. It's an excellent fund for retirees taking monthly distributions.

It's No Secret

According to the Vanguard Model Portfolios historical data, a 30 percent stock/70 percent bond split will return about 7.3 percent. We use 7.3 percent as our primary benchmark to evaluate our overall portfolio performance. Our returns for each of the last three years was 13.9% (2009), 10.6% (2010) and 2.5% (2011). We outperformed our benchmark two of the three years. Nothing far-fetched. These returns are within the range of expected performance between the returns of the broad stock market and the Barclay's Bond index. This is reasonable with low risk and low costs.

The principle reason our portfolio grew the last three years was the broad stock and bond market rallies after the 2008 crash. Stocks stalled in 2011 but not bonds. Why did bonds perform so well in the last three years?

Recall when the Federal Reserve (or the bond market) lowers interest rates the value of existing bonds increases. Since the 1980s the Federal Reserve lowered interest rates. In the last three years due to the sluggish economy they have been aggressive and persistent. In January, 2012, the Fed announced it would not raise interest rates until 2014 sending yields on new bonds even lower. We have never before heard of the feds so committed to keeping low interest rates.

We live in a low interest rate era, the lowest we experienced. When we bought our Los Angeles home in 1981, interest on the third trust deed was 17 percent. 1981 was a different era.

With 70 percent of our portfolio allocated to intermediate-term bonds, the net asset value (NAV) increased as a result of the feds pouring money into the financial system since 2008 while keeping interest rates low. This is partly why bonds may be overvalued and why our portfolio value increased the last 3 years.

There may be another possibility why bonds increased in value. Since 2008 millions of investors have been seeking a flight-to-safety by putting their money into money markets and bonds for consistent performance and safety, albeit getting minimal interest. Investors are also loading up their portfolios with potentially risky long-term maturity bonds because they are chasing higher yields erroneously thinking there is little or no risk. Many investors don't understand chasing long-term bond yields may backfire when interest rates increase. We know our intermediate-term bonds will decrease too, but do the long-term bond holders know they are taking greater risks than we are?

Knowing this risk we compromise by buying intermediate-term bonds with slightly lower yields. The yield is lower because of its lower risk -- which also fits with our plan. We gained by buying bond funds before the 2008 crash when they were not as expensive as now.

Is it possible we are in another bubble--a bond bubble? There has been a lot of chatting about this. Bonds' NAV are at their all time highs. Look at the NAV of your bonds and you will see they are probably near their historic high. We don't want to pay high prices for anything, stocks, bonds or even a pair of matching sweaters. We want them on sale. Thus, we direct the interest payments from our bonds into stock funds and into cash. With our Vanguard account we set this up automatically. We're not reinvesting the quarterly interest payments and yields of our bonds to purchase new bond shares. No way—bonds are too expensive. At the end of each quarter bond interest payments are fed into a money market account until the accumulating sum can be either reinvested in stock funds or spent.

In 2004-2006 when we overhauled our investment allocation to include bonds we had no idea bonds would do well. No one can predict which asset class will perform best. For sure the market doesn't know. We used no gimmicks, found no gems, avoided active manager gurus and used no secret formulae for our portfolio performance the last three years. We received market returns from stocks and bonds. A 100 percent diversified stock portfolio might be fine for a 20-something millennia generation investor but isn't appropriate for two retirees in their 60s and 70s. To try to catch up by taking on more risk because of past investing mistakes is a mistake unto itself.

We survived two massive crashes. Throughout this past decade from 2002 to 2012 we didn't abandon our efforts to put our economic house in order with a new foundation. Our recovery shows it's possible to rebound from mistakes, financial loss and restore savings in a safe, practical and disciplined way.

In the next chapter we share 18 years of financial growing-up backed up with data: what we invested in and how we evolved into a couple of do-it-yourself late-bloomers. How does our portfolio compare to Vanguard Wellington and Steve's pension plan's performance all of those years?

CHAPTER 8

How'd We Do?

(1994-2011)

With 18 years of records to answer this question we compare our portfolio performance with the major market indicators: the NASDAQ, Barkley's bond, S&P 500 and the EAFE indexes (Europe, Australia, Far East). We also compare our portfolio with Steve's pension plan, California State Teachers Retirement System (CalSTRS) and two other funds—Vanguard Wellington and Paul Merriman's "Ultimate Buy & Hold" portfolio.

The results of these comparisons might surprise you. We thought our mistakes wrecked our financial future. We were wrong. If you don't make the same mistakes and implement what we discovered from Bogle's work you will increase the likelihood of achieving your financial goals.

The data and the figures show the effects of our misguided tech bubble overconfidence, lack of diversification and the subsequent positive mid-course corrections in our portfolio over 18 years. Taken over almost two decades those errors of judgment and inexperience morphed into valuable lessons which offer insight on the strategies we learned and applied.

Prior to 1994 we were methodical savers in a combination of annuities and managed funds. We stopped all annuities and started investing in no-load mutual funds in 1994. Dan was 53 and Steve was 47, not exactly novitiates. Our long-term habit of investing half of our pay raises and tax refunds and Steve's V.A. benefit for his Vietnam injuries increased our contributions. By 1994 we accumulated $223,977 from our tax-sheltered annuities and savings including Dan's lump-sum payout of $38,000 from his California State University pension plan. With this money we created our first no-load mutual fund portfolio.

Our average savings rate was approximately $12,500 per year from 1976 until Steve retired in June, 2008. At the beginning we saved little and gradually increased contributions. That average includes all income sources: rental income, retirement payout, Steve's V.A. payment, et al. As salaries maxed at the height of our working careers we invested twice our average rate.

Figure 9 shows our first stock market peak in the context of all of the data from 1994 through 2011. The amounts show the value of our portfolio at the end of each year, including our contributions and dividends with fees subtracted. 2000 was the time for Dan to become a gentleman of leisure — retired. We felt great all of those years leading up to March, 2000, but then fell into a maddening descent from an imperious high to humble beginnings. It fell on us like an unreinforced brick wall during an earthquake.

We picked ourselves up from the financial rubble, dusted off and retooled. Figure 9 may be the most informative graphic in the book. It shows the long-term benefit of tenacity. Incredible as it seems we ended up in 2011 with the same nest egg value we achieved in 2000.

Figure 9 leads directly into many of the concepts we discussed in our story. Now we have data to back up a discussion of the following topics:

- Long-term thinking
- Consistent contributions and sticking with a plan
- The effects of volatile returns
- Comparisons to benchmarks
- Comparisons to California State Teachers Retirement System (CalSTRS), Vanguard Wellington and Paul Merriman's "Ultimate Buy & Hold"
- Value and small-cap tilted investing

The figures are created with Excel. We downloaded our data from the Morningstar.com (M*) "portfolio" feature. Recall from an earlier chapter we used M*'s tool to track holdings and retrieve the data illustrated.

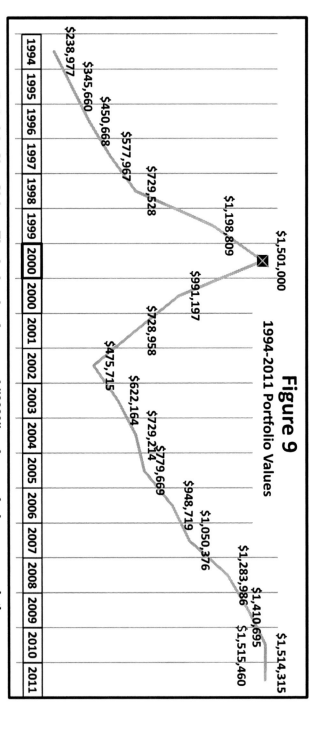

Figure 9
1994-2011 Portfolio Values

$238,977
$345,660
$450,668
$577,967
$729,528
$1,198,809
$1,501,000
$991,197
$728,958
$475,715
$622,164
$729,214
$779,669
$948,719
$1,050,376
$1,283,986
$1,410,695
$1,515,460
$1,514,315

| 1994 | 1995 | 1996 | 1997 | 1998 | 1999 | 2000 | 2000 | 2001 | 2002 | 2003 | 2004 | 2005 | 2006 | 2007 | 2008 | 2009 | 2010 | 2011 |

End of the Year Values. The darken border around "2000" and upper dark square mark the March 10, 2000 technology bubble peak of our portfolio. The next 2000 is end of the year.

Each year we tallied the new shares reported by the mutual fund company statements, inserted the data into the portfolio and printed the M* report. These reports turned out to be essential for illustrating how the portfolio behaved and evaluating the performance with industry benchmarks.

Long-term Thinking

The relationship of long-term thinking and investing success is as interdependent as orchestral instruments resonating toward a symphonic crescendo. At the end of 35 years of retirement planning many would be pleased to earn one and a half million at the height of two working careers. We didn't sell at the market top *or* bottom. Neither did we abandon the market, even though we felt it abandoned us. We continued to contribute for the long haul: chastened, but not bitter. How did we do it?

We learned proper diversification including the vital bond allocation matching our age. As a result of this simple balance, the market and our portfolio recovered. It was a slow go and we were patient after the first crash. With Dan becoming a househusband in 2000, Steve kept contributing and took a second weekend teaching position to broaden employment skills while adding to the retirement pot.

You might ask, "why didn't you sell at or near the top, in March 2000 and avoid all of the stress and pain of losing?" We didn't know and neither did anybody else. There are always juxtaposed financial optimists and gloomy prognosticators who will be right half the time. Like most people, once we decided our chosen sector could only go up, we pooh-poohed evidence to the contrary. We would have sold and rebalanced if we knew the market topped and would be crashing and if we knew what a diversified portfolio looked like.

Think about the 2012 stock market. As of April, the Dow and S&P 500 index posted their best first quarterly returns since 1998. The NASDAQ composite gained nearly 19 percent in its strongest launch since 1991. Our portfolio gained about $60,000 in the first quarter alone. This was great news and it felt wonderful *at the time*.

However, who could say the market is at its highest after today's close? Who could say the market will crash tomorrow, continue to fall for the next few months and stay down for the next decade? You can find impeccably dressed professionals who can argue persuasively either way. Japan has not rebounded from their astronomical stock market high for 22 years. Could it happen here? Who knows? Past returns are useless for predicting trends. We all know that, and yet, delusional attempts at predicting persist.

A mystifying question is why many people sell at the bottom when prices are low. When the market is high there's no rush to sell. This scenario happened in March 2000. We didn't get out for the same reason most investors don't sell at the high. The mass exodus happens when markets drop 20 percent or more. Panic selling at the bottom provides Wall Street the opportunity to scoop up your shares, hoping to sell them back to you at their profit, once you get past the queasy stage.

Our portfolio would not have recovered as much as shown in Figure 9 had we panicked. Instead, we gradually diversified into low-cost indexed mutual funds to get back on track. By 2004 each trade was planned and executed as we gradually transferred into index funds using the passive strategy. We eschewed risky "catch-up" investments, those touted gems which appeal as shortcuts to wealth.

Investors and many professionals forget the long haul as their worried minds allow doom and gloom thoughts. Individuals with a fabulous low-cost plan and competent adviser will still be psychologically challenged by a shaky market. It's a cinch to stay put when the market goes up but difficult or impossible to sustain long-term thinking when the market goes down. All of the good planning, hard work and thinking seemingly go out the window not because money was lost. Instead, long-term thinking vanishes likes roaches to a kitchen light.

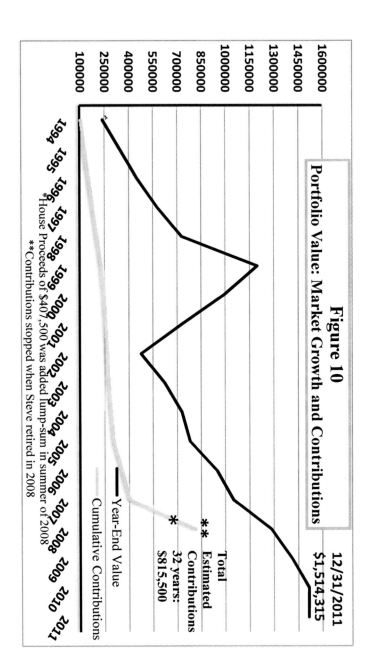

Figure 10

Portfolio Value: Market Growth and Contributions

	12/31/2011
Total	$1,514,315
** Estimated Contributions	
* 32 years:	$815,500

— Year-End Value
— Cumulative Contributions

*House Proceeds of $407,500 was added lump-sum in summer of 2008
**Contributions stopped when Steve retired in 2008

Thirty-two years of Contributions

Figure 10 combines our cumulative contributions as a light gray line and the annual portfolio values in the stark black line. The 1994 starting point of $105,000 is based on our memory, an estimate of 403(b) annuity contributions and after tax savings from 1976 to 1994. We use $223,977 as an estimate of prior contributions and earnings ($118,977) from the annuities, thanks to higher interest rates through the 1980s.

From 1994 to 2008 our contribution record is a close estimate. The graph shows the *accumulated* contributions to 403(b) plans, Roth IRAs and after tax investing. In 2008 our final contributions include Dan's small inheritance from his dad, the house proceeds and Steve's last 403(b) contribution to TIAA CREF. After 32 years we saved about $400,000 (plus our home sales proceeds) despite mistakes and a "late start."

Volatile Returns

The NASDAQ composite follows the highly volatile technology industry sector. Because so many investors, including us, were seduced by this sector in the late 1990s and early 2000s, we took a closer look at this relationship. Figures 11 show the returns of our portfolio from 1994-2011 and Figure 12 shows a comparison of the portfolio with the NASDAQ returns.

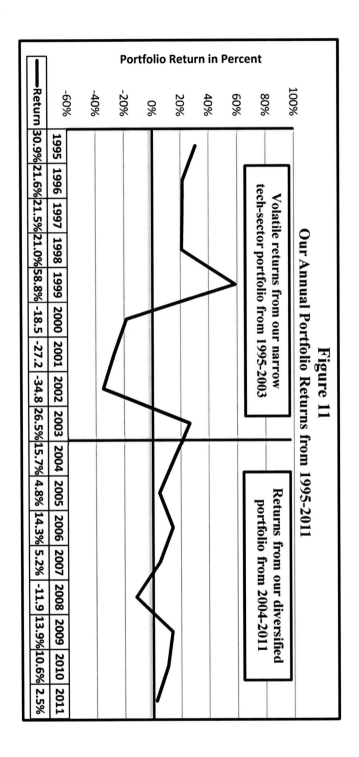

Figure 11
Our Annual Portfolio Returns from 1995-2011

Portfolio Return in Percent

Volatile returns from our narrow tech-sector portfolio from 1995-2003

Returns from our diversified portfolio from 2004-2011

	1995	1996	1997	1998	1999	2000	2001	2002	2003	2004	2005	2006	2007	2008	2009	2010	2011
Return	30.9%	21.6%	21.5%	21.0%	58.8%	-18.5	-27.2	-34.8	26.5%	15.7%	4.8%	14.3%	5.2%	-11.9	13.9%	10.6%	2.5%

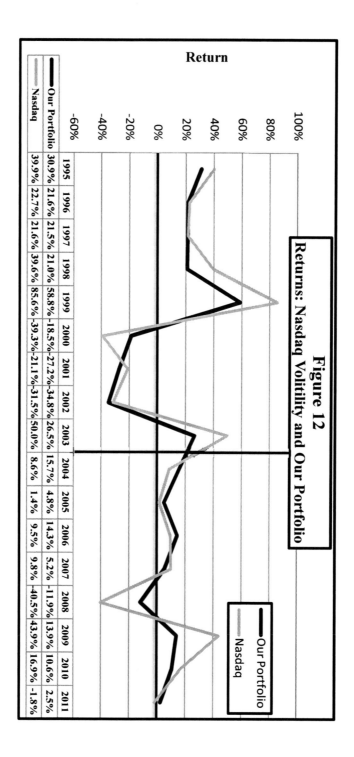

Figure 12

Returns: Nasdaq Volitility and Our Portfolio

	1995	1996	1997	1998	1999	2000	2001	2002	2003	2004	2005	2006	2007	2008	2009	2010	2011
Our Portfolio	30.9%	21.6%	21.5%	21.0%	58.8%	-18.5%	-27.2%	-34.8%	26.5%	15.7%	4.8%	14.3%	5.2%	-11.9%	13.9%	10.6%	2.5%
Nasdaq	39.9%	22.7%	21.6%	39.6%	85.6%	-39.3%	-21.1%	-31.5%	50.0%	8.6%	1.4%	9.5%	9.8%	-40.5%	43.9%	16.9%	-1.8%

In both figures the left side shows the returns of the tech sector funds and individual stocks we owned. Notice the extreme annual ups and downs. This is what investors *must* avoid. The right side of the vertical line shows the returns of a diversified portfolio. With the excessive churning and volatility on the left of the vertical line we lost all of the gains, more than a million dollars. Roller coasters are exciting and terrifying when our money is riding with us, flying into the wind and lost forever.

None of our portfolio returns from 2004 through 2011 were above or below 16 percent. Our porridge was the right temperature. The 2008 banking/insurance/mortgage crises caused a huge hit affecting all asset classes. We were lucky to lose "only" 11.9 percent. Many investors lost more than 40 percent, including NASDAQ aficionados.

It's still amazes us how closely our portfolio reflected the NASDAQ returns through most of the 17-year history of the data. After we diversified out of the narrow NASDAQ into the broad market indexes and bonds the volatility dropped like a freshly-born Holstein calf from its standing mother. The NASDAQ continued its volatile ways, crashing about 40 percent in 2008, then soaring with a 43.9 percent gain in 2009. This latest volatility was a repeat performance of the tech bubble. We slammed on the brakes and stopped the excessive up and down madness. The portfolio and its owners matured, now acting like the grown-ups in the room.

Benchmark Comparisons

Figure 13 shows how the portfolio compares with the EAFE international market, the S&P 500 Index and Barclay's Bond indices.

Frequently yesterday's darlings become today's wallflowers. After the NASDAQ love-fest the next darling everybody loved in the 2000s was international stocks, *especially* emerging markets. The EAFE outperformed the other indices and our portfolio four straight years (2003-2007).

Then came 2008. You guessed it. The EAFE *under performed* the other indices with a huge decline of -43.4 percent. It was EAFE's turn to become the "wallflower" from 2009 through 2011. 2011 was another double-digit negative year with a 12 percent loss.

The international indices *still* have not recovered at this writing. Our Vanguard International Stock Index has remained below its summer 2008 high when we invested some of the house proceeds. At the time we allocated seven percent in international stocks as planned, *not* because of market conditions. Since 2008 we bought emerging markets to rebalance into that beaten down inexpensive asset class to further diversify our international core holding.

Barclay's bond index performed as it should with a steady and predictable return of about seven percent over seventeen years. On the right side of the vertical line our returns are higher than the Barclay's bond index and below most equities, where our portfolio is supposed to be.

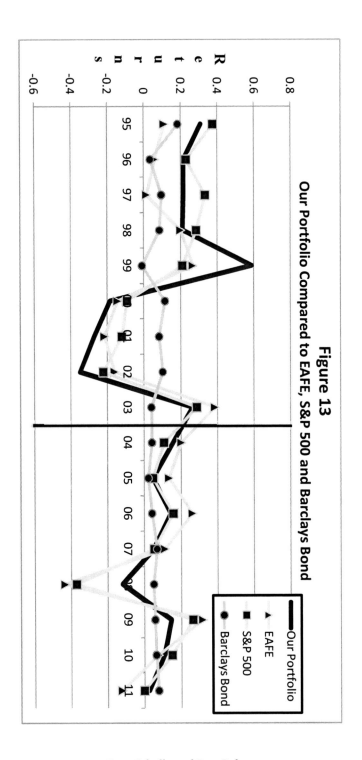

Figure 13

Our Portfolio Compared to EAFE, S&P 500 and Barclays Bond

Steve Schullo and Dan Robertson

Remember to always look at your portfolio as a whole. Don't be tempted to get all verklempt over one specific fund performance. Most of all, don't try to predict the next darling which will eventually break everybody's heart—treat them the same by investing in *all* of the darlings.

Vanguard Wellington, California State Teachers' Retirement System (CalSTRS), Paul Merriman's FundAdvice Ultimate Buy & Hold Portfolio

The next approach to answer the question of "How'd we do?" is to compare how we did to professionally designed and managed portfolios. We selected portfolios which are frequently discussed on investment forums and websites devoted to individual investors and reported in the media. We wondered about our original choice for years—Vanguard Wellington.

Recall when Steve was informed his original 403(b) choice, Wellington, was not available in 1993. The dismissive comment from his employer was the seminal experience leading to his jihad to improve 403(b) options for educators. If Wellington *were* available back then, how would we have fared?

Figure 14 shows what our nest egg would be worth hypothetically, if we put our contributions into Wellington (VWELX). We also include CalSTRS and Merriman's "Ultimate Buy & Hold" portfolios returns for instructional asset allocation contrast: stock/bond split with corresponding risk and return, value and small-cap tilt (discussed shortly).

Figure 14

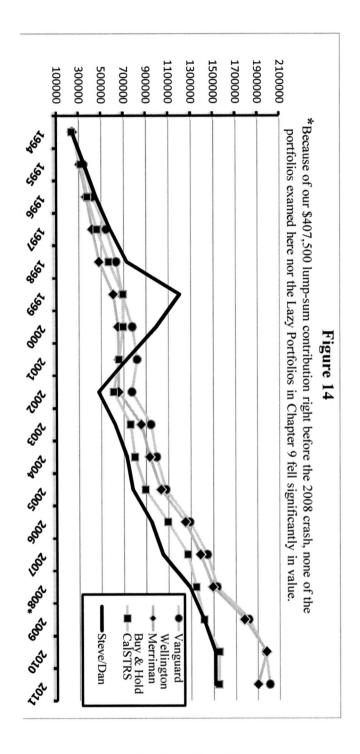

*Because of our $407,500 lump-sum contribution right before the 2008 crash, none of the portfolios examed here nor the Lazy Portfolios in Chapter 9 fell significantly in value.

The returns are published on their respective websites. We calculated the returns based on the same contributions shown by the light gray line in Figure 10 and compared the results from each portfolio in Figure 14. The figure shows an expected result and a surprise. First, Wellington returned an impressive $1,937,928, $423,613 more than our own. This is expected given we made mistakes and learned along the way. Second, Wellington outperformed CalSTRS by almost as much! Now that's surprising.

Value and Small Cap-Tilt

When we showed these results to a friend who is familiar with the CalSTRS investment policy he asked, "How did Wellington do so much better than CalSTRS?" Yes, it's a great question. Here is what we think happened.

The academic financial community has conducted numerous studies which show that for over 80 years value companies (companies which pay dividends) outperform growth companies (young fast growing companies, often technology stocks). Value stock average annual returns are a few percent more than the stock market as a whole, over time—a huge return difference.

Let's compare Vanguard Wellington's (Figure 15) and CalSTRS' (Figure 16) asset allocations. Wellington's allocation has not changed from its basic stock/bond split (63 percent/37 percent) over the years. Wellington invests sixty-three percent in value-oriented companies with thirty-seven percent in bonds and fixed assets.

This allocation worked well through the two recent stock market crashes.

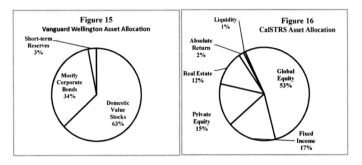

CalSTRS is a different story. Through most of its 95-year history CalSTRS had 100 percent bonds. Starting about 30 years ago the managers turned from risk averse to an overly risky allocation by holding 82 percent equities. A huge turnaround in one generation. An 82 percent equity allocation is extremely risky for any portfolio other than for someone younger than 30. In 2008 they suffered a 26.2 percent loss, their worst in history. But CalSTRS is hardly alone.

Wellington suffered a 22 percent loss in 2008. Due to its 36 percent corporate bond allocation and its focus on domestic large-cap value-oriented stocks, Wellington grew steadily during our time frame. It gained during two of the three years in the dot com crash whereas CalSTRS lost ground during all three years (2000-2002). Wellington did so well it outperformed all the other professionally designed sample portfolios we illustrate in the next chapter. One fund: Paul Merriman's "Ultimate Buy and Hold" portfolio would have returned $1,819,393, slightly less than Wellington.

Steve Schullo and Dan Robertson

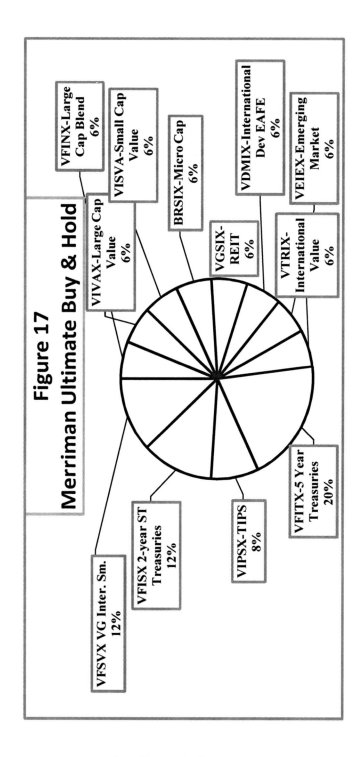

Figure 17
Merriman Ultimate Buy & Hold

VFINX-Large Cap Blend 6%

VISVA-Small Cap Value 6%

BRSIX-Micro Cap 6%

VDMIX-International Dev EAFE 6%

VEIEX-Emerging Market 6%

VIVAX-Large Cap Value 6%

VGSIX-REIT 6%

VTRIX-International Value 6%

VFSVX VG Inter. Sm. 12%

VFISX 2-year ST Treasuries 12%

VIPSX-TIPS 8%

VFITX-5 Year Treasuries 20%

As it turns out Merriman's stock/bond split is almost identical to Wellington—36% bond. As a result both lost less than CalSTRS. Figure 17 shows the "Ultimate Buy and Hold" asset allocation. Merriman's allocation holds 36 percent bond with a value tilt too: 24 percent value-tilt and 16 percent small and micro-cap. Small-cap companies outperform large caps by a similar 3-4 percent margin according to academic research. This allocation helps explain Merriman's standout portfolio performance.

Our Allocation (2008-Present)

Figure 18 shows the overall basic stock/bond/cash allocation of our current portfolio.

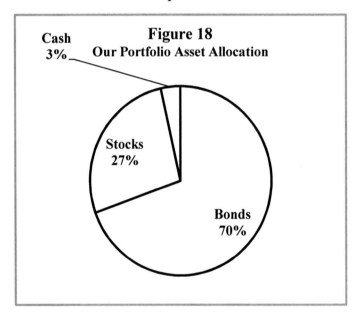

Figure 18
Our Portfolio Asset Allocation

Cash 3%

Stocks 27%

Bonds 70%

While this overview is a guideline, Appendix B shows a detailed allocation and a rationale for the funds we chose.

For several years we erroneously figured mistakes would doom us to play catch-up. Our portfolio performed slightly below Steve's pension plan--not shabby. These results convinced us our mistakes were not as bad as we thought. If two educators with no financial training can do this, so can you. We invite you to embark on an investing journey, renewed and encouraged.

Disclaimer: None of the graphs in this book are peer reviewed or based on original research. The simulated portfolio performances are made possible due to two Bogleheads: dubbed Simba and TrevH on the Bogleheads investment forum. They created an Excel program for dozens of asset classes with returns dating back to 1972 with 25 different Lazy Portfolios. They invited people to use the program to back test the different Lazy Portfolios and asset allocation configurations for our education.
We used their Excel program to back-test our data for the graphs we created for Vanguard Wellington and Ultimate Buy and Hold (We calculated the CalSTRS results by hand) in this chapter and the next using our contributions and distributions. We use the Excel program with its Lazy Portfolio returns with our contributions from 1994-2011 for illustrative purposes only. Do NOT change your allocation solely based on any of the graphs or data presented anywhere in this book without financial education and without understanding risk. This data is for educational use only. The benefit of comparability provides real-life examples to compare performance, gain insights about different asset allocations over different time periods. Past returns have never been a guarantee of future returns.
Our application revealed the two high performing portfolios: Vanguard Wellington and Ultimate Buy and Hold: their performance is specific to the past and nothing more is assumed— this applies to all of the Lazy Portfolio data presented in the next chapter. There are multiple factors which are impossible to replicate in the same or similar way in the future. If we promised similar results we would be as delinquent as advisers who promise specific returns. To download Simba's Excel program for your own analysis of your portfolio, log on to: *http://www.bogleheads.org/wiki/Simba's_backtesting_spreadsheets.*

Part Three
It's Your Turn

"Lazy Portfolios give investors a far
superior alternative than gambling
retirement savings in Wall Street's casino.
Simple solutions: Just three to 11 no-load
low-cost index funds, and zero trading."

—Paul Farrell, MarketWatch,
March 27, 2012

Steve Schullo and Dan Robertson

CHAPTER 9

Your Plan

Setting up a simple plan or simplifying your current portfolio

After reading our story we are confident you are inspired to start. Since we are all getting older and wiser anyway, let's do ourselves a favor—plan for it. "It's never too late," says Jack Brennan, former Chairman and CEO of The Vanguard Group.

This chapter shows how uncomplicated it is. If you already have a portfolio you can tidy it up, streamline and refocus your clutter of individual stocks and sector funds. We aren't promising anything far-fetched. Even though we're not certified financial advisers, what we discovered isn't elusive or scary. Building wealth starts with knowledge, tools, patience and commitment. This chapter shows how thinking long-term, controlling costs and consistent contributions to a diversified plan are compelling. This will *reduce*, not eliminate, risk and uncertainty.

Lazy Portfolios

The simplest plans are dubbed lazy portfolios. John Bogle started with the S&P 500 index and many variations of indexes followed. Modern Portfolio Theory (MPT) specifies diversification to reduce risk and increase returns. Eugene French and Kenneth Fama examined 80-year historical data and found higher returns came from value stocks over growth stocks; small-cap outperformed large-cap stocks. With these three developments: passive management strategy, MPT, and French/Fama research. The lazy portfolios synergize these essentials and strategies. Additional reading about this research and each lazy portfolio author presented in this chapter is located in the reference section.

William Bernstein conducted his analyses and provided insights about index portfolios in his highly regarded books *The Intelligent Asset Allocator* and *The Four Pillars of Investing*. His comprehensive analyses of how portfolios are constructed support the lazy concept. Finally, Scott Burns chimed in with his lazy portfolio version which he coined the "couch potato."

In the last decade numerous authors designed additional versions for the ordinary investor. Imagine these individuals sitting happily on Burns' couch, a Marge Carson sofa, chatting about family, friends, traveling, anything other than talking shop. They, like us, want to live and not worry about trying to beat the market or find the next hot investment gem. Their lazy portfolios serve us, not the valueless industry traders, so we can also enjoy our couch without financial worry.

Investing should be dull, investing should be more like watching paint dry or grass grow. If you want excitement, take $800 and go to Las Vegas.
—Nobel Economist Paul Samuelson.

Lazy Portfolios are exactly what Dr. Samuelson's quote advises—each is an unexciting portfolio sans micromanagement. As we said throughout this book excitement is not part of the slow-as-you-go investing experience. Recall how excited we were when our portfolio grew a half million in four months at the height of the dot com bubble. Listen to this emotion— it's as clear as "the long roll" of a Civil War drummer— we took too much risk.

We list 10 lazy portfolios containing two to seven funds. Each has a brief explanation and a pie chart of the asset allocation. The returns include dividends and the expense ratios have been deducted. Finally, we constructed a graph showing back-testing analyses of how each of the lazy portfolios would have performed with our contributions from 1994 through 2011. We compare those results to what we actually earned.

With the exception of Harry Browne's Permanent Portfolio, the other examples adhere to Bogle's original indexing strategy, creating varied indexed versions.

Compared to our volatile start from 1994-2004, each lazy portfolio returned smooth and ongoing growth with minimal losses through two major crashes. Isn't that how low-cost, broadly diversified, passively managed stock and bond portfolios with little trading are supposed to work? Of course.

Don't you just love it? You are about to find out how fortunate we are to have these great thinkers looking out for our best interests.

Scott Burns' Couch Potato

THE DUPLEX ©2012 Glenn McCoy. Dist. By UNIVERSAL UCLICK.
Reprinted with permission. All rights reserved.

Burns created his couch potato portfolio in 1987. He writes personal finance articles for numerous news organizations and runs a management firm called AssetBuilder. His nine couch potato portfolios are on his website. Most use Vanguard indexes and start with simple to more complex asset classes. We only illustrate his original because of space limitations. Scott believes we don't need to waste valuable time trying to beat the system—we can *still* outperform investors who believe they can.

His couch potato invests half of an investor's assets in Treasury Inflation Protection Security (TIPS) and half in the total stock market index. That's it. This portfolio would be an excellent start for newbie investors of any age. Had we invested our money using this portfolio, rebalancing each year, we would have about $138,530 more than what we earned and with a lot less volatility and risk.

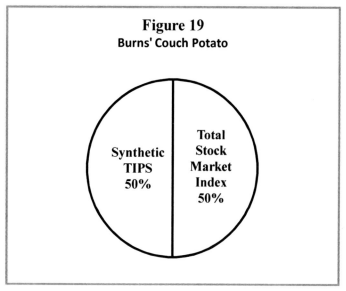

Figure 19
Burns' Couch Potato

Synthetic TIPS 50%

Total Stock Market Index 50%

Note: Synthetic TIPS are estimated returns calculated before 2000 when TIPS were not available. In the illustrations presented, the synthetic TIPS returns were used from the Excel program discussed in the disclaimer. However, from 1994-2000, the actual returns were used for 2001 to 2011. Taken over 18 years, we assume that the TIPS returns used are reasonable for our illustrations.

If you're lazy or just plain not interested, you can actually get by with only three asset classes, and thus, three mutual funds: the total U.S. stock market, foreign stocks, and short-term bonds. That's it—done.

William Bernstein, Author.

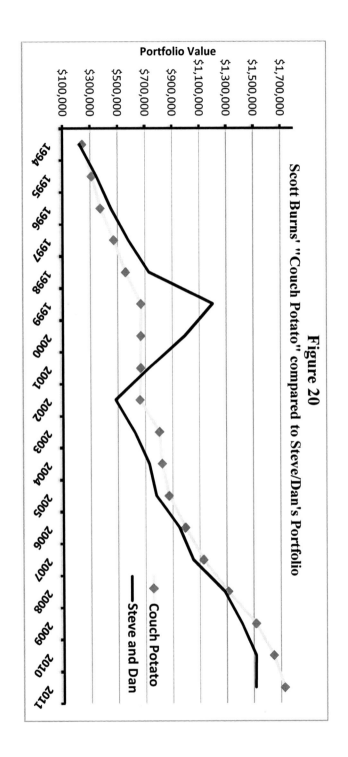

Figure 20

Scott Burns' "Couch Potato" compared to Steve/Dan's Portfolio

Portfolio Value

$1,700,000
$1,500,000
$1,300,000
$1,100,000
$900,000
$700,000
$500,000
$300,000
$100,000

1994 1995 1996 1997 1998 1999 2000 2001 2002 2003 2004 2005 2006 2007 2008 2009 2010 2011

◆ Couch Potato
— Steve and Dan

The next portfolio has three funds. Adding the Total International Index (VGTSX) expands the range of stocks from the United States to the rest of the world. This broad-based addition includes emerging markets (Asia and South America). Why would anyone want to add another fund? We want to further diversify our risk as much as possible, i.e., spread it out between disparate asset classes.

Taylor Larimore's Three-Fund Portfolio

Taylor Larimore co-founded Morningstar *Vanguard Diehards* and the *Bogleheads.org* investment discussion forums. He co-authored two books devoted to the Bogleheads investing philosophy.

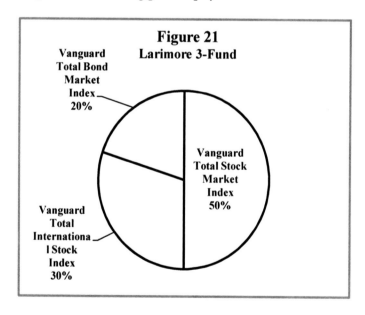

Figure 21
Larimore 3-Fund

Vanguard Total Bond Market Index 20%

Vanguard Total Stock Market Index 50%

Vanguard Total International Stock Index 30%

Larimore's portfolio would have returned $48,776 more than we did. What is impressive is how the portfolio recovered from the 2008 devastation when it lost 30.74 percent and came right back with a 26.56 percent gain in 2009. Too volatile for our purposes—retired and over 60 years old—been there, done that.

To be fair Taylor would advise, as Bogle does, late starting and older investors should increase the total bond market allocation to one's age. Our 70 percent bond allocation was the main reason why our portfolio fell a modest 11.9 percent in 2008.

Steve Schullo and Dan Robertson

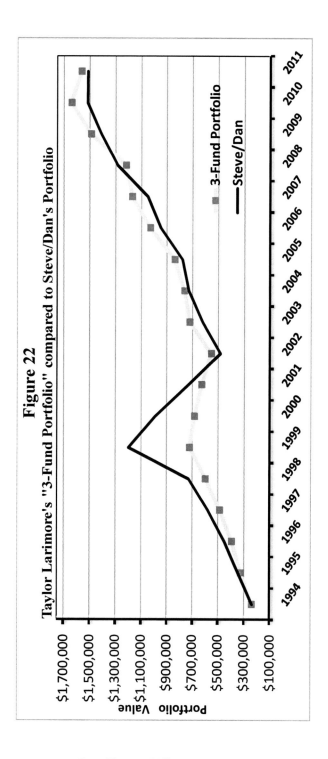

Figure 22

Taylor Larimore's "3-Fund Portfolio" compared to Steve/Dan's Portfolio

Allan Roth's 2nd Grader

Kevin, Allan Roth's son, an 8-year-old second-grader started investing with a gift from grandma and a few hints from dad. This is another uncomplicated starter portfolio with three no-load funds.

Our dissertation project advisers counseled us to explain our research projects so simply a 12-year-old could understand. If you believe 12-year-olds cannot understand investing, think again.

This father-son team replicated this timeless transfer of knowledge from the older generation to the next, just as Steve understood owning 3M stock from his mom who purchased her employer's stocks. With modeling and examples of how the process works, investing is *not* complicated.

The costs are low, it's diversified, it's simple and rebalanced annually—this remarkable second grader's portfolio held up with a 90 percent stock allocation, but not without volatility. This allocation is risky—the stock/bond split should be used by young investors with a long time horizon, under 35 years old. If you are older, increase the bond allocation. As expected, the returns and the volatility are similar to Taylor's portfolio.

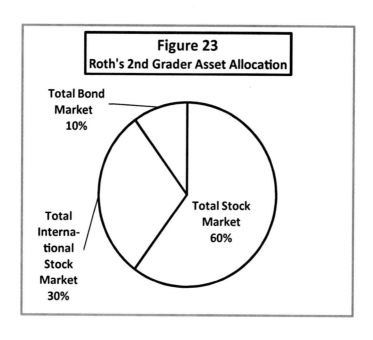

Figure 23
Roth's 2nd Grader Asset Allocation

Total Bond Market 10%

Total International Stock Market 30%

Total Stock Market 60%

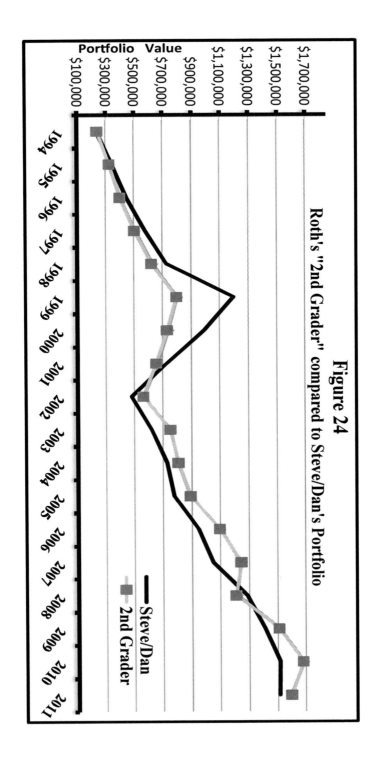

Figure 24

Roth's "2nd Grader" compared to Steve/Dan's Portfolio

The remainder of the Lazy Portfolio examples add more asset classes. When you are ready to add more funds you can refer to the following portfolios as a guide to include value, small-cap-tilt, REITS and even gold.

Rick Ferri
The Core Four Portfolio

Rick Ferri's core four portfolio includes an eight percent allocation to REITS (real estate investment trusts). It's another asset class option. Ferri's core four funds drive the primary return, but he encourages the user to tweak the portfolio with small percentages of other funds.

Ferri authored numerous books on the passive strategy including the popular *All About Asset Allocation* and his latest, *The Power of Passive Investing: More Wealth with Less Work*. He is the founder of the low-cost management firm, Portfolio Solutions. He finds the time in his busy schedule to help people online with finances, free of charge, as a regular and courageous contributor to Bogleheads.org investment forum. He's a straight shooter with his financial advice for us regular folks and professional peers.

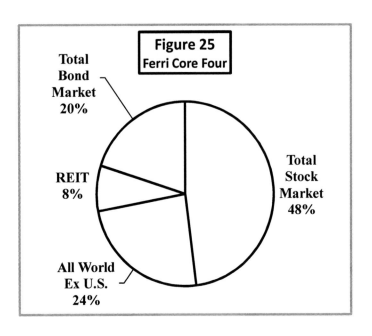

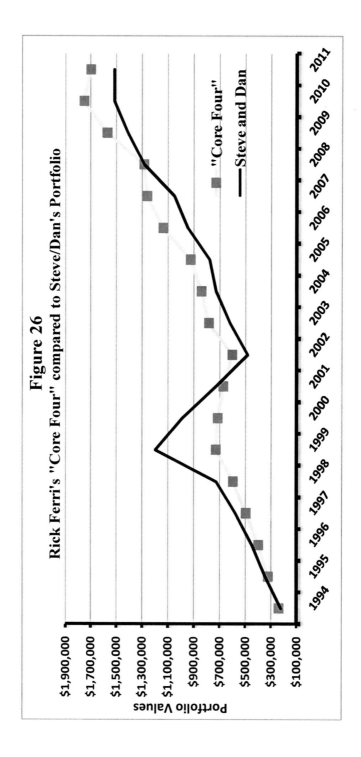

Figure 26
Rick Ferri's "Core Four" compared to Steve/Dan's Portfolio

Harry Browne's Permanent Portfolio

The "All Weather" portfolio is designed for investors who believe a financial Armageddon may be around the corner—geopolitical shocks, sudden financial failures of national economies, war, revolution, natural disaster, or massive stock market crashes resulting in either hyper inflation or deflation.

The basic premise is to divide investments into two parts: 1. The *usual* holdings for the lazy portfolio family, Vanguard Total Stock Market Index and the Treasury Money Market and, 2. The *unusual* holdings: 25 percent in long-term bonds and 25 percent in gold.

Fifty percent in non-core investments is risky. Gold is an alternative investment outside of the standard asset classes. The maintenance schedule is the same as all lazy portfolios: rebalance, keep simple, with reasonable returns while ignoring the noise.

Browne's portfolio outperformed ours by an impressive $265,196. In the last ten years long-term bonds and gold helped this portfolio. Long-term bonds performed well in the last five years as many investors chased the relatively higher bond yields, driving long-term bond prices higher along with the Federal Reserve stimulus plans. The upward trend hasn't stopped at this writing. Gold delivered double digit returns from 17 percent to 30 percent in seven of the last ten years. The flight to safety in gold and long-term bonds propelled Browne's portfolio. The "lost decade of stock investing" in this new century propelled gold and long term bonds.

Figure 28 shows the portfolio started to outperform us in 2008 and took off in the last three years. Similarly our portfolio blew the roof off of *all* the lazy portfolios in the 1990s tech bubble. When a portfolio has a fifty percent allocation in two sectors (gold and long-term bonds) which outperform the broader markets that portfolio would be expected to outperform too.

We don't count on an Armageddon-type scenario to meet our financial goals. For the record we invest in gold and long-term bonds in the total stock market index and in the total bond index, respectively. We believe in exposure to these two investments, only not as much as Browne.

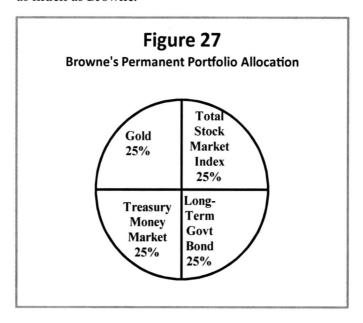

Figure 27
Browne's Permanent Portfolio Allocation

Gold 25%

Total Stock Market Index 25%

Treasury Money Market 25%

Long-Term Govt Bond 25%

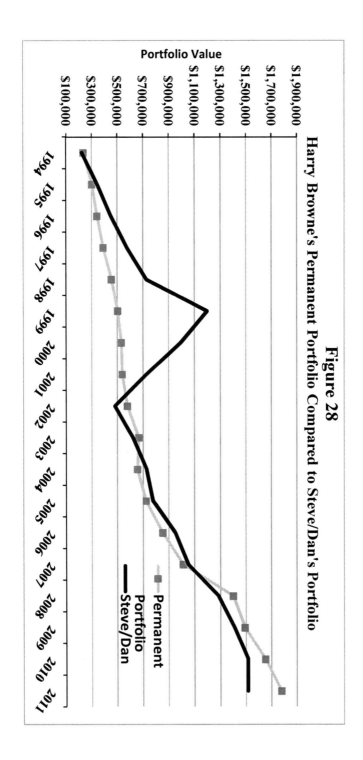

Figure 28

Harry Browne's Permanent Portfolio Compared to Steve/Dan's Portfolio

Steve Schullo and Dan Robertson

Dr. William Bernstein wears many hats: physician, neurologist, author of several excellent financial books and financial adviser to high-net-worth individuals. This one is also simple: Allocate 25 percent in each of four index funds diversified across basic core asset classes. This portfolio tilts towards developed countries (no emerging markets exposure).

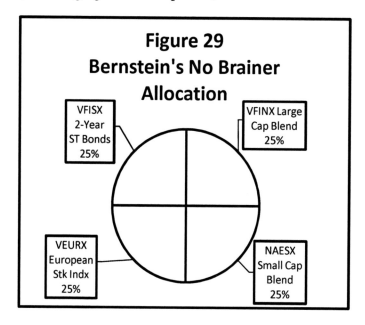

Figure 29
Bernstein's No Brainer
Allocation

VFISX
2-Year
ST Bonds
25%

VFINX Large
Cap Blend
25%

VEURX
European
Stk Indx
25%

NAESX
Small Cap
Blend
25%

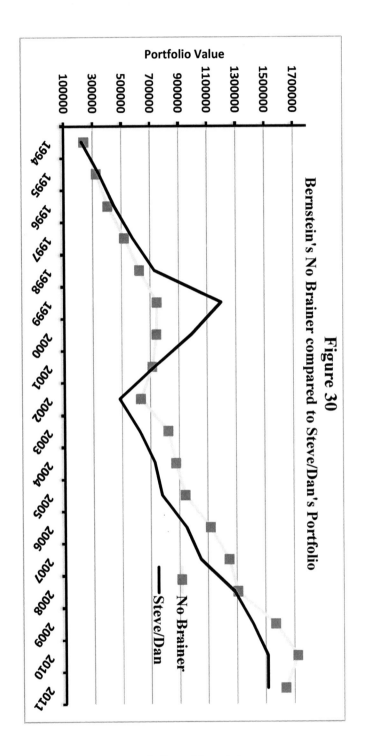

Figure 30
Bernstein's No Brainer compared to Steve/Dan's Portfolio

Steve Schullo and Dan Robertson

David Swensen's Lazy Portfolio

Mr. Swensen is the long-time manager of the Yale University Endowment Fund and author of *Unconventional Success*. He suggests this portfolio for the average investor. It outperformed us by $165,000. What do you think accounted for Swensen's excellent record?

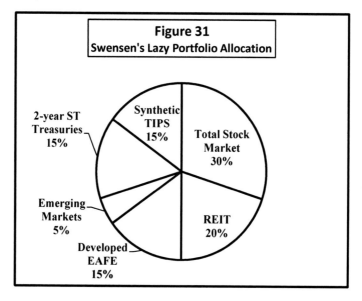

Figure 31
Swensen's Lazy Portfolio Allocation

2-year ST Treasuries 15%

Synthetic TIPS 15%

Total Stock Market 30%

Emerging Markets 5%

Developed EAFE 15%

REIT 20%

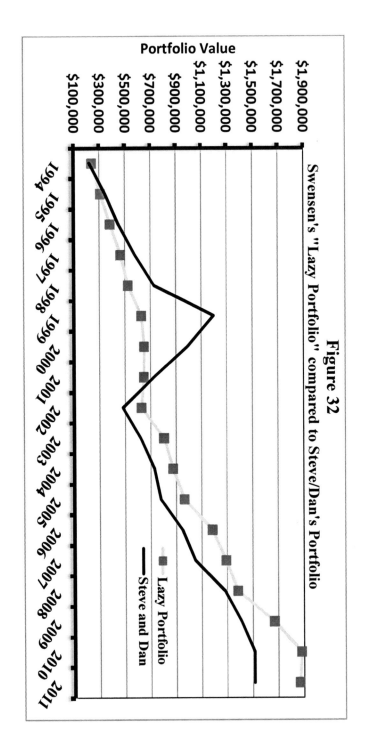

Figure 32

Swensen's "Lazy Portfolio" compared to Steve/Dan's Portfolio

Frank Armstrong's Ideal Index

Armstrong also believes index funds eliminate active managers' risk. He's overweight in small-cap stocks with a value tilt because of the historical return data established by previously mentioned research.

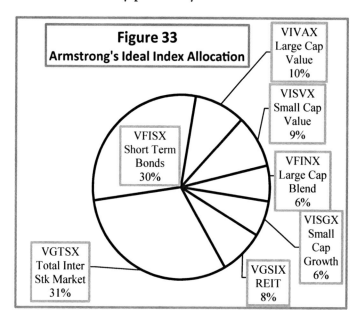

Figure 33
Armstrong's Ideal Index Allocation

VIVAX Large Cap Value 10%

VISVX Small Cap Value 9%

VFINX Large Cap Blend 6%

VISGX Small Cap Growth 6%

VGSIX REIT 8%

VGTSX Total Inter Stk Market 31%

VFISX Short Term Bonds 30%

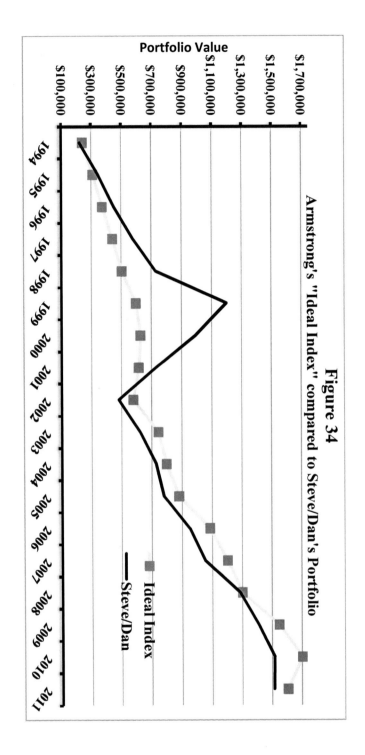

Figure 34
Armstrong's "Ideal Index" compared to Steve/Dan's Portfolio

Steve Schullo and Dan Robertson

Larry Swedroe Simple Portfolio

Swedroe's portfolio equals the S&P 500's gain with less volatility thanks to a healthy stake in bonds and a value-tilt with small cap exposure. Once again, this allocation outperformed our portfolio just shy of $200,000.

Larry Swedroe is the director of research for St. Louis-based Buckingham Asset Management. Along with Rick Ferri, Swedroe is another frequent contributor with free advice on the Bogleheads forum and is a prolific author: *What Wall Street Doesn't Want You To Know* and his latest, *The Quest for ALPHA: The Holy Grail of Investing.*

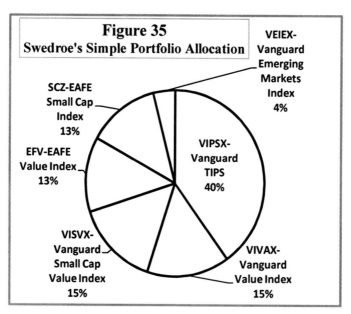

Figure 35
Swedroe's Simple Portfolio Allocation

VEIEX- Vanguard Emerging Markets Index 4%

SCZ-EAFE Small Cap Index 13%

EFV-EAFE Value Index 13%

VIPSX- Vanguard TIPS 40%

VISVX- Vanguard Small Cap Value Index 15%

VIVAX- Vanguard Value Index 15%

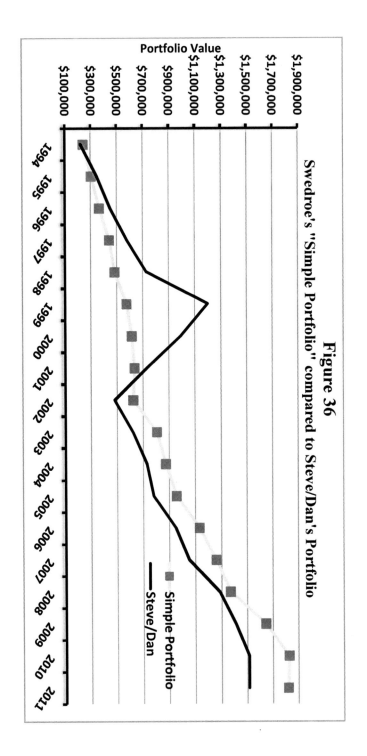

Figure 36

Swedroe's "Simple Portfolio" compared to Steve/Dan's Portfolio

Steve Schullo and Dan Robertson

Bill Schultheis Coffehouse Investor

We are fond of Bill's website: *How to build wealth, ignore Wall Street and get on with your life.* Bill's Coffeehouse Investor allocation comes closest to our asset plan. Our allocation to bonds is higher at 70 percent but the equity diversification is similar. All of the asset classes are represented. We also enjoy our daily brew especially *Peets Coffee and Tea.*

Bill is a principal and fee-only financial adviser with Sound Wealth Management. His popular book, *The New Coffeehouse Investor* is in its third edition.

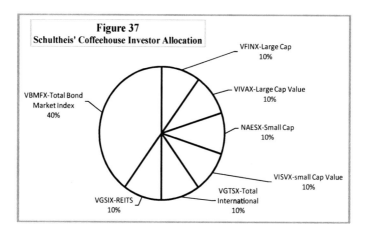

Figure 37
Schultheis' Coffehouse Investor Allocation

- VFINX-Large Cap 10%
- VIVAX-Large Cap Value 10%
- NAESX-Small Cap 10%
- VISVX-small Cap Value 10%
- VGTSX-Total International 10%
- VGSIX-REITS 10%
- VBMFX-Total Bond Market Index 40%

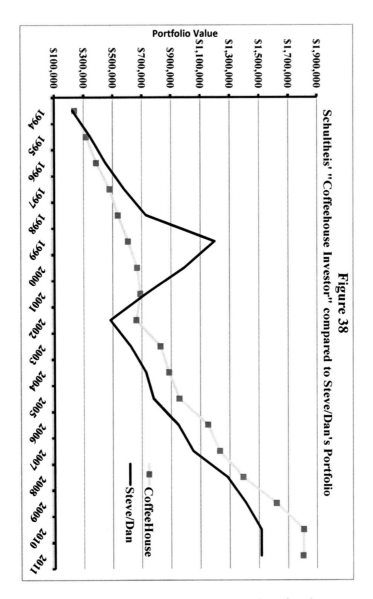

Figure 38

Schultheis' "Coffeehouse Investor" compared to Steve/Dan's Portfolio

The lazy portfolios provide a template for the rest-easy investor. They have pristine performance over the long haul through good and negative markets. We hope you found them helpful.

Summary

Still not sure you can start your own lazy portfolio? We know the feeling—it took us a while too. But, you have a clear advantage: technology, transparency and objective information with improved and low cost investment choices available now. We believe that any of these portfolios or the additional ones on each author's website will get you started.

This chapter shows a variety of ways to embrace and apply the low-cost indexing principles. You can get started immediately if you are eligible for the Roth IRA (just about everybody is who earns a wage). However, your employer's sponsored tax-deferred retirement plan might not be cooperative. Low cost indexes are often not available in 401(k), 403(b) and 457(b) plans. In the next chapter we tackle several related road bumps or issues you might run into and suggestions to encourage your employer to offer a lazy portfolio.

Steve Schullo and Dan Robertson

CHAPTER 10

Demystifying Your Employer's Plan

Understanding your employer's tax-deferred retirement plan can be one of life's mysteries. A variety of asset classes, authors and their model portfolios were introduced in the last chapter to help. Your two challenges:

1. Find any of the lazy portfolio funds available in your employer's plan.

2. If your employer has a lousy plan, petition to make low-cost indexes available.

If your employer has the total stock market index, total international stock index and a total bond market index available with total fees less than 1.0%, you can skip this chapter. This chapter is for folks with mediocre and expensive plans or who want to assist their spouse or friend with their lousy plan.

When we began our search 20 years ago we didn't

have the lazy portfolio examples. The first lesson we learned was to *never* pay commissions. This one absolute has two applications—retirement plans and investing. We avoided commission loaded annuities and mutual funds. We searched for no-loads. This initial information was plenty for us to get started.

Recall how frustrated Steve was in his pursuit of requesting a simple list of no-load mutual funds from his employer, LAUSD, in 1993. Times have changed due to Internet access streamlining your research. Steve volunteers on the district's committee overseeing the 403(b) and 457(b) plans. His district has finally offered information online. Now you may find it easier to get a copy of your employer's plan, it's quite another to recognize if it's a decent plan.

Employers' Tax Deferred Retirement Plan

The starting place for your retirement savings is your employer's sponsored plan. Tax deferment makes the payroll savings plan compelling. Automatic deductions into your funds will result in a W-2 reflecting those savings. Your taxes will be reduced -- payable when the money is taken out in retirement.

Total fees over 1 percent in an employer's sponsored plan are too expensive and reduce the advantage of the tax-deferred benefit. Figure 40 in Chapter 11 (page 198) shows how 1.35 percent in fees cost thousands of dollars over just a few years, using our portfolio as an example.

Investment Policy Statement (IPS). Large companies with 100 or more employees who offer retirement plans have an IPS. It's provides rules for emergency withdrawals, transfers, loans, costs and other pertinent details. Does your company's plan have a broker such as Schwab with access to multiple funds? LAUSD's 457(b) plan offers a TIAA-CREF Brokerage Services option, a self-directed window for hundreds of investment choices. If you hire a financial adviser, the IPS is an important document to show him or her for a fresh perspective to set up your individual plan.

Does the Following Scenario Sound Familiar?

Often salespeople show up at your place of business unannounced with contrived apologies or barely bridled enthusiasm. They offer free lunches arranged by the union rep, boss or other supervisory person. Your co-workers mean well and want to do the right thing, but they are often clueless.

"Ah," the boss may think, "this is an opportunity to offer a plan for everyone which costs nothing to the company and the employees." This offer becomes the salesperson's plan, not the boss's or yours. You're set up for a costly and inappropriate plan.

When the salesperson tries to pitch their investment products we say, "Thanks, but no thanks, I have a plan, *my own*." Don't expect them to congratulate you.

Approaching the Boss

According to the Census Bureau about 40 million Americans work for small businesses employing fewer than 100 people. Since there are so many people in this category we think it would be important to discuss in detail how Dan approached his boss to offer a quality, low-cost employer's tax-deferred plan. Recall Dan started a new 403(b) at his non-profit job with a few phone calls and signatures.

As a new employee at the Van Ness Recovery House, Dan asked his boss about 403(b) options. He learned her predecessor invited an agent who enrolled several employees into a large insurance company annuity. Nobody used it anymore: investing had stopped along with servicing this account. With permission from the boss, Dan contacted Fidelity and T. Rowe Price and started an accessible plan with many options.

The paperwork was easy. It didn't involve the boss. Dan signed the forms, received and distributed the promotional packets and encouraged colleagues to save. About five out of the twelve total employees signed up, a high percentage considering the relatively low salaries. This didn't require a séance with somebody in a suit -- a few simple phone calls were all it took.

His boss was happy because she got the plan too and didn't have a new administrative task. The payroll company knew how much to send to the mutual fund companies backed by each employee's written request. Those companies distributed the money received into the individual funds selected by each participating employee. Not a difficult program to implement for small for-profit or non-profit organizations.

Vanguard was not on Dan's radar yet. It seemed too tame and he was put off by the idea of "passive" investing. "Why not go for the gold?" he figured. We now laugh about his thinking 20 years ago.

For The Small Business Employer

If you're the owner, consider an option of increasing the match in the company's 401(k) plan in lieu of a raise. When raises are automatically saved to 401(k)s, participation increases significantly. A behavioral science study by UCLA researchers called "Save More Tomorrow" supports the idea that people don't like their paychecks reduced when they start to save. As a result, they put it off. The study found that it's tolerable when the deduction is in lieu of a raise—it's vital that take-home pay remain the same. People don't like their hard-earned wages "taken away" but are comfortable with pay raises automatically invested in long-term savings.

Small company plans are less complex to set up and run than large company 401(k) or 403(b) plans. For small businesses tax-deferred retirement plans can be launched with low-cost funds such as Vanguard, TIAA-CREF or Fidelity or another low-cost company. You aren't on the hook for these plans because they're between employees and the fund companies. Vanguard, for example, has a portion of their website set up with a live person to help you. The Simple IRA is designed for small businesses with few administrative demands. It's an awesome benefit you can provide. Matching contributions are also a business tax deduction (employer matches are not required in 403(b) and 457(b) plans).

Some employees want more information. They can call any company you decide to use (hopefully low-cost) and talk with a consultant. The Employee Retirement Income Security Act (ERISA) protects the assets of millions of Americans so funds placed in retirement plans during their working years will be there when they retire. The Department of Labor website has the ERISA guidelines.

For Large Employers (more than 100 employees)

Large companies will probably have to set up an official 401(k) plan and hire a third party administrator (TPA) and a financial consultant. The TPA's and the consultant make sure it complies with ERISA guidelines. Consider forming an oversight committee and ask your employees to participate. LAUSD asked Steve to join the newly formed Oversight Committee as a voting Member-at-Large.

The LAUSD's oversight committee includes a nonvoting financial consultant, third party administrators, and voting member employees from: collective bargaining units (teachers, administrators, custodians, staff, school police, etc.), Chief Financial Officer, a representative from the board of education and LAUSD's benefits administration. The benefit's administrator serves as the chair and one of employee members is the co-chair. Having the employees share in some of the decisions is one surefire method to keep the plan in compliance.

Brightscope.com is a resource for businesses of all sizes for both the employer and the employee. It rates

401(k) plans from poor to excellent on costs, matching, investments, participation and total assets. If you're the employer you can locate a financial consultant to assist you in setting up a plan. At this writing, it's beginning to rate 403(b) plans.

The Internet Came to the Rescue
for Us Working Stiffs

Because of the Internet, finding plan information isn't an excruciating ordeal any longer. After reading this chapter and checking out the resources at your disposal you are armed with enough information to recognize excellent, mediocre or dreadful retirement plans.

Don't be surprised if your employer offers a lousy and expensive plan. Pre-K-12 school districts are notorious for having only expensive and inappropriate 403(b) insurance products available. The challenge is to petition for low-cost lazy portfolio funds. Steve devotes a second book to this subject alone. For now, we will provide a brief introduction to advocacy.

How to Petition your Current Employer

Inform the person responsible that you are requesting a low-cost, no-load fund. Some companies have an oversight committee. Attend a meeting and make your request. Be specific, polite but firm. Take an example of one of the lazy portfolios as a visual illustration of what you are requesting and why: costs, diversification, stock/bond split, market returns over time. Explain how costs eat into your nest egg. For a clear explanation of costs, show Appendix D to the person responsible for the company's benefit plan.

If you have a union or association, attend your collective bargaining unit meeting and make your request in the form of a motion. Your union usually has a retirement or a finance committee of your colleagues to facilitate your request.

If your employer or union won't assist, you can open an IRA (Individual Retirement Account) on your own. Check your eligibility since not everyone can participate in an IRA. The tax-deferred benefits are the same as any company qualified plan and the amount deferred is confirmed by the IRA mutual fund and reported by you or your tax adviser when you file your 1040. Call their 800 number for the forms. Most mutual fund companies require a minimum investment, often $3,000.

Professional consultants to large company employer sponsored plans are beginning to admit costs matter to investors. Heightened sensitivity to Wall Street tomfoolery, particularly leading to the 2008 crisis, is countered by the positive influence of Bogle and his followers as evidenced by Vanguard's $1.7 trillion in assets. Your request may not be perceived as a threat to Western Civilization like it was in Steve's experience. He no longer feels marooned as a voice for common sense. In fact, your chance of getting a low-cost option honored has increased significantly.

Steve had to compromise to get a no-load mutual fund charging 12b(1) fees instead of Vanguard Wellington. This isn't the best approach but it's a start as you continue to push for that low-cost plan from your employer. Compromise is an option but your effort to press for low-cost options is *never abandoned*. It took Steve ten years to get TIAA-CREF into his employer's plan (It was a different era than today). He selected TC immediately for his 403(b) contributions in the last six years of his working career. Fidelity signed up too. It's a worthy pursuit even though your colleagues may never know how fortunate they are for your advocacy. Doing the right thing is the ultimate reward.

Lifestyle and Target Date Funds

One of the best creations for newbie investors who don't want to touch their investments or hire a fee only adviser is to use Lifestyle or Target Date Funds. Both do the same thing. The concept is sensible: the fund managers reduce the risky part of the funds as your retirement target date approaches. They hold the approximate proportions of the stock/bond split to meet your time horizon and risk tolerance. Vanguard's lifestyle funds consist of various established index funds.

Target date funds are popular choices with 401(k) and 457(b) plans. Chances are your employer has a target date fund available. If not, ask them to get one. Make sure the fund chosen has reasonable costs. You might have to work a little harder to get them in your 403(b) plan.

We talk cost all through the book, maybe ad nauseam. Once again some of the available target date funds cost over 1 percent. That's way too much. You shouldn't pay so much when there's so little to manage. Vanguard Target Date funds typically cost .18 percent -- that's practically nothing. If you hate to touch your portfolio a Target Date fund might be right for you.

Roth IRA Option

Roth IRAs are an excellent long-term option and don't require your employer's permission. Most Americans who earn a wage can use the Roth IRA. What a great option – it really delivers and you can start with one of the lazy portfolios immediately. How neat is that?

Ordinary income taxes are paid first. The Roth can grow dividends and capital gains as tall as a hybrid corn field at fall harvest. In retirement the money is *all yours* and can be taken out tax-free.

It should be another core holding in all portfolios, reducing taxes in retirement. We invest about 10 percent of our portfolio in a Roth. The only downside is a maximum annual contribution of only $5,000 if you are younger than 50 and $6,000 if you are 50 or older. There are additional high-net-income individual restrictions (2012). Most income earners easily qualify for the Roth IRA, but check with your tax professional for all tax questions.

Free at last!

For You and Your Tax-Deferred Savings Plan

You just retired. Congratulations. Take time to adjust to a daily routine you now control. It takes several months to wind down from the demands of working and transition to activities you are now free to do 24/7.

One of the first things on your new list is to liberate your money. Don't delay getting your money out of your former employer's plan and roll it over into a rollover IRA. We did our rollovers so all our funds are easier to track. Your greatest advantage is that you will save a bundle in costs. You are free to use any of the lazy portfolios, which cost less than most employer sponsored plans.

Steve Schullo and Dan Robertson

CHAPTER 11

The Case of the Missing Fiduciary

Lazy portfolios are one answer to reducing costs for investment products. Now we turn our story to locating a financial adviser for services and advice. Where is the trusted and competent advisor who looks after our best interests and at low cost? Our adviser is close by, perhaps closer than we think.

We will be looking through the daunting maze of the intimidating financial culture to find ethical assistance. We'll need a roadmap for our journey to find who fits our need for objective information, similar philosophy and long-term growth. Financial advisers come in all flavors, skills and beliefs. We consider these topics in our search:

- Our "tipping points" with financial advisers
- What is a fiduciary?
- Identifying Inappropriate Investments

- Mutual Fund Advisers
- Avoiding product-driven advisers and agents
- Sales pitches versus objective financial information
- Management Costs
- Fee-Only Adviser
- The Missing Fiduciary

Our Tipping Points

Recall from the introduction we asked our respective advisers about mutual fund 403(b) options. Dan's adviser said he would "help," salivating as he realized a potential commission. Steve's question about mutual funds to one of his advisers was repulsed as abrupt and fierce as a midwestern thunderstorm.

Steve's other adviser was worse. She simply ignored his request for a change. He asked for a product with no surrender charge. She plied on Steve's naiveté by putting him into a different insurance company with a surrender fee he specifically said *he did not want*. Later during the process of transferring these TSAs to a mutual fund Steve paid surrender fees to *both* companies totaling $6,000. While he never experienced divorce this "case" was a messy breakup with two insurance companies and a huge "alimony." These surrender fees pay the company back for the commissions paid to this despicable adviser.

Many professionals decry this type of sleaze. Some argue one bad apple doesn't spoil the entire basket. This may be true in normal life. In the surreal 403(b) world, however, advisers' accountability is rare and their actions are not just dripping with conflicts of interest but pouring like that thunderstorm.

The surrender fees were Steve's tipping point. He was so livid about those fees he wanted to write a book. Today, 20 years later, he's honored by this opportunity to spread a positive message and to protect others from similar hucksters.

What is a Fiduciary?

According to Wikipedia, *A fiduciary is someone who has undertaken to act for and on behalf of another... he must not put his personal interests before the duty, and must not profit from his position as a fiduciary, unless the principal consents.* A fiduciary is a legal term requiring professionals to put their clients' needs and interests ahead of their own. Fiduciary standards occupy a position of special trust and confidence.

These standards include, but are not limited to: *disclosure of compensation and any corresponding potential conflicts of interest.* Fiduciary duty has been on the financial regulation books for more than 70 years after The Investment Advisers Act of 1940 passed Congress and was signed by President Roosevelt. This bill addressed some of the corruption, insider stock trading and other conflicts of interest leading to the 1929 stock market crash and the Great Depression.

If fiduciary duty has been on the books all of these years we would think it would be easy to find a fiduciary. Unfortunately it's not that simple. Fiduciary responsibility has always been held by Certified Public Accountants (CPA) and attorneys. In the financial management profession however the legal definition is more complex and often ignored. The industry has systematically mucked up a fair and clear definition of a responsible fiduciary.

Complexity is one of this industry's greatest assets. Some financial professionals have fiduciary responsibility with official certification such as a Certified Financial Adviser (CFA) and Registered Investment Adviser (RIA). Brokers in broker/dealer firms are not certified or fiduciaries, the suitability standard says the investments shall be "suitable." Please tell us what suitability means? It gets worse…in our profession as educators where insurance retirement products are sold by the billions of dollars, insurance agents are responsible to their companies, themselves or to their businesses, not to educators.

While Congress and state legislators aim at a specific target to regulate, the industry moves it a bit. And that's all it takes. The rationale is straightforward. Finding and exploiting loopholes in proposed bills is the lobbyist's wet dream with handsome rewards waiting. For example, insurance products do not qualify as securities under the securities act; thus, a person who sells them is not required to be a fiduciary.

Recently when Congress looked into the inclusion of insurance products as securities, the industry fought hard and stopped that effort. If the industry gets wind of proposed regulation the lobbyists know months ahead to block it or find loopholes. And they're good. This effort is not just confined to the financial industry. It's standard practice in our modern political system protected by first amendment rights, especially with plenty of money and power.

In our opinion, forget what's happening with the federal regulations recently passed and signed into law. Insurance agents and their products are masterfully excluded from those parameters. Furthermore the idea of fiduciary responsibility has unintended consequences complicating our search. At their professional meetings the industry has workshops on fiduciary responsibility. *Everybody* is calling themselves a fiduciary. Imagine that, it's the new *in*-word for sales pitches and presentations. This popular self-description now trumps transparency.

It's a perfect example of an industry which knows ahead of time how to counter proposed regulations as new investments and products are developed, presented and sold.

Most of us enter the investment business for the same sanity-destroying reasons a woman becomes a prostitute: it avoids the menace of hard work, is a group activity that requires little in the way of intellect, and is a practical means of making money for those with no special talent for anything else.

—Richard Ney, ***The Wall Street Jungle***

We want an advisor whose fiduciary responsibility is to us, not to his or her company, the lobbyists, state insurance commissioners, campaign war chests or the origin of it all, Wall Street. The answers are fairly straightforward—in our opinion discover how to evaluate your current adviser or potential adviser and their products to assure he or she is acting in our best interests better than any regulation.

Avoid Product-Driven Agents and Advisers

Expensive retirement products with the accompanying sales pitches are easy to recognize. Our initial agents were thinking, "I only know about my products, so don't bother me with your questions about mutual funds." Their allegiance to products rather than to answering our questions is crystal clear. And why not? Eighty percent of all educators in 403(b) plans buy fixed, variable or indexed annuities. In the largest school district in California, the second largest in the nation, for example, $2 billion are in Tax Sheltered Annuities (TSAs). The steady flow of millions of dollars in annual fees from about 55,000 former and current employees to the companies resemble hundreds of dairy cows in a mindless procession through the milking station three times a day, seven days a week.

Why would our agents change for us? For half a century agents had easy pickings selling annuities to preK-12 teachers. What are the products the agents love but are bad for us? In our opinion the insurance industry shouldn't be part of any employer's tax-deferred retirement plan during the *accumulation stage*. (Low-cost annuities may be appropriate for a guaranteed income stream in the *distribution stage*). For starters, TSAs have no added tax benefit in qualified 403(b), 457(b) and 401(k)s as reported by the Security and Exchange Commission (SEC) in 2000.

Annuities versus Equities

Fixed or indexed annuities shouldn't be confused with long-term growth investments such as the lazy portfolios. The price for never losing money and the resulting peace of mind is difficult to comprehend. Lazy Portfolio returns are *never* guaranteed—a primary advantage. Annuity products guarantee never to lose money, while not informing people that neither will you beat inflation in low performing "safe" products. In order to pay for any guarantees, annuities are "capped" so returns in higher performing investments are never realized by the annuitant. "Never-losing-money" in a restrictive annuity contract is the primary reason why many unsuspecting people purchase annuities—it provides the sales pitch and rationale for keeping people from thinking while escalating fear of the stock market and exploiting it for the deal. Jim and Mary Toohey wrote: "…fear of stocks is way overblown. We need them because of their superior returns…." We agree.

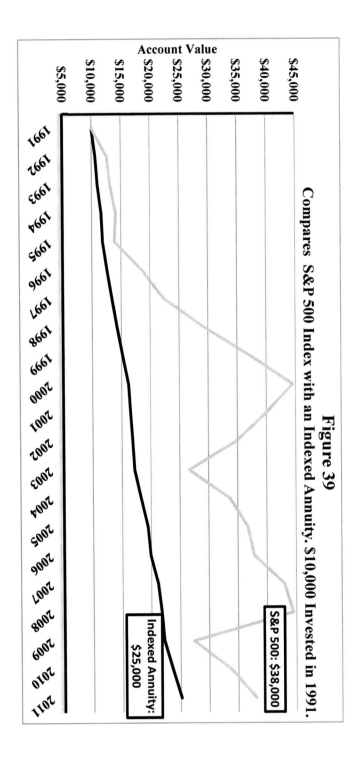

Figure 39

Compares S&P 500 Index with an Indexed Annuity. $10,000 Invested in 1991.

S&P 500: $38,000

Indexed Annuity: $25,000

Figure 39 Note: Past returns of the S&P 500 index are thoroughly vetted and well publicized. But the past returns of annuities are rarely publicized. The annuity performance in this graph is an estimate and it should not be used to generalize to other types of annuity contracts. There are hundreds of different contracts with as many different maximums and minimums available.

Figure 39 shows how the limitations of the contracts are why stock market equities beat annuity returns over long periods of time. The contract agreement is the controlling factor for how much the insurance company decides to give the annuitant, *not the stock or bond market*—this is a major disadvantage of annuities for long-term growth. The stock market has little to do with annuity returns—the insurance company decides how to credit annuitants.

> *Reject the comfortable tyranny of the fear of losing.*
> *Embrace the freedom of losing the fear of losing.*
> **—The Authors**

The difference in value of the two accounts ($13,000) is what an annuitant will *not* get from 1991-2011. The "not getting" is the price for this riskless contract. Annuities are constructed to give you a pittance during bull markets and no losses during bear markets. In this example, even when the annuity provides a two percent *gain* during the two massive losses suffered by the S&P 500, a $10,000 initial investment underperformed the S&P by $13,000 after twenty years. This money pays for the commissions, pizzas and donuts to sign up more clients. It's *rarely* understood.

The product is a contractual agreement with the

insurance company, *not an ownership investment,* such as a stock mutual fund. Agents see us as potential commissions and move on to the next sale. The insurance agent and their product are conjoined. Neither of these Siamese twins is a fiduciary, nor a long-term ownership investment.

Subjective vs. Objective Financial Information

We learned in school the subjective and objective dichotomy for understanding complex concepts in science and other subjects. Subjective comments originate from emotions in an all or nothing view: "*You* will lose money in the stock market!" Subjectivity provokes an emotional reaction.

Objective comments originate from independent evidence, hardly emotional, "A lazy portfolio is broadly diversified to reduce stock market risk." Objectivity is neutral and informational.

We use the "compare and contrast" analytic tool for deconstructing the language used in subjective sales pitches versus objective information. Recognizing objective financial information will greatly help us in our search for the illusive fee-only adviser. In the financial industry objective information is our one best friend—this alone helped us clear away the daunting maze of endless financial information to find the good stuff—it's crucial. But what exactly is objective financial information? Table 13 compares sales pitches with objective information.

Table 13
Compare and Contrast Line by Line (continued next page)

Sales Pitches	Objective Information
1. "The company pays my fees."	1. "My fee is $200 per hour." (Or another specific fee per hour).
2. "This product is *suitable* for you."	2. "I will help you set-up *your plan*."
3. "I *guarantee* X percent returns for X number of years."	3. "Future returns are *unpredictable*. There are no guarantees."
4. "I can double your money *in ten years* with guaranteed rates."	4. "The goal is to build wealth *slowly over a working career*."
5. "And you have a death benefit *included*."	5. "For death benefits, purchase a *separate* term life insurance policy."
6. "Don't *worry about my costs*. The higher returns will pay for them."	6. "You will pay an expense ratio of each fund. But *we will keep those costs low* with the index investing.
7. "You don't want to be average. You want to beat the averages!"	7. "We will set up a broadly diversified index portfolio that will generally *follow market averages* using Vanguard, TIAA CREF or Fidelity."
8. "We guarantee that you will not lose money from your principle."	8. "TIAA CREF's Traditional Annuity offers a *low-cost fixed account*. No surrender fees and no loss of principle."

Table 13, continued
Compare and Contrast Line by Line

Sales Pitches	Objective Information
9. Phone: "Hi, I am calling you because my company has a new product to transfer your money. It's a great product that will do better than the one you have now."	9. "I will only make transfers if it's part of your original retirement plan to rebalance as needed."
10. "We use complicated quantitative analysis that will help predict market downturns or bull markets and change your portfolio strategy in anticipation of major market fluctuations."	10. "Market timing relies on luck. Relying on luck is not a strategy. I will help you stick with your original plan during good and especially during bad economic times. No complicated analysis can predict the future."
11. "You get what you pay for because our service is superior to those low-cost companies like Vanguard. All you get with them is an 800 number."	11. "As your adviser with fiduciary responsibility my job requires me to look after your best interests by helping you get and stay diversified with low cost funds and stick with your plan."

The two columns reveal a clear difference in tone. If you attended a financial presentation complete with a free lunch or dinner you might recognize the comments in the left column. They are emotional and intentional. In contrast the right column has useful information with no halcyon promises. Now we are getting somewhere—*recognizing objective information.*

Fiduciary advisers use the objective information in the right column and act accordingly. The sales people say anything from either column to land a sale and do little afterwards. It doesn't take an MBA to discover which column reflects both adviser behavior and information serving our best interests. An expanded inventory of short-term thinking and sales pitches versus long-term thinking and objective information is presented in Appendix C.

Sales pitches are intentionally vague to create complications and exploit fears. They keep people unfamiliar with finances and supplant naiveté with artificial trust. When people trust the sales person to deliver what is promised—peace of mind, the goal of all insurance, the deal is closed. A straightforward easy manner is essential to earn trust and a doughnut helps.

We purchase insurance in the appropriate places—home, auto, earthquake, long-term care and umbrella insurance from our folksy homespun agent. We are pleased to pay $5,000 per year for insurance premiums. Insurance companies protect our indispensable personal belongings against loss. Likewise, a lazy portfolio is an appropriate long-term investment. The two should *never* be mixed in the accumulation stage.

Mutual Fund Advisers

Perhaps you don't worry about high cost insurance products because your adviser would agree with us about annuities. You might be thinking "I met my adviser at church (or at the union hall) and she prides herself on selling mutual funds." Just clarify what you are paying in total costs to both the mutual fund company and your adviser. If you are paying less than 1 percent per year in *total costs*, with a lazy portfolio type plan, you are OK. You are also fortunate.

Most advisers have no financial incentive to put you in any low-fee company. While you now know Vanguard and TIAA-CREF charge no commissions, 12b (1) fees or high annual expenses, other independent firms or brokerage houses will add a fee(s). There are hundreds of for-profit financial firms and independent advisers who don't share Vanguard's or TC's client-centered corporate cultures. While you might be earning market returns the conflict of interest and the high costs erode your returns.

Steve chatted with a "Union-Approved" adviser about his clients at a United Teachers-Los Angeles (UTLA) meeting. The adviser knew Steve abhorred annuities and told Steve, "I never sell annuities. I hate them too." The adviser worked as a mutual fund adviser for a national broker/dealer securities corporation. (UTLA subsequently terminated the decades old union-approval policy in 2008).

One evening this gregarious and portly middle-aged potentate informed Steve, upon his query, "I have 350 union members as clients." Steve said, "That's a lot of clients," and asked, "How much does each one of your clients have in their portfolio?" He said he didn't know. So let's assume some numbers for illustrative purposes.

- Let's imagine his 350 clients with an average of $65,000 invested.
- 350 X $65,000 = $22,750,000 under his watch.
- If he or the company charges an assets under management (AUM) fee of one percent, .01 X $22,750,000 = $227,500 could be his estimated annual gross revenue for the corporation he works for and himself.

We don't know how much of this revenue the adviser would share with the corporation. This adviser's salary includes possible additional commissions for signing up new clients. Then there are those little devils in most managed and loaded mutual funds, the 12b(1) fees which are additional costs for marketing. They pay the adviser, corporate administration and profits for the shareholders. This company serves their sales personnel, employees and itself first. Where do the interests of the 350 teachers lie within this gauntlet of corporate pickpockets?

Could this "advisor" have opportunities to suggest transfers within each of these 350 accounts? Transfers, also known as churning, are expensive for investors because of additional charges. Our financial adviser may earn a *conservative* $150,000 or more per year, more than twice the average teachers' salary.

Despite this potential annual income a larger question remains: How in the world can one adviser take care of 350 clients' individual needs? If every client had no more than $65,000 in their portfolio it is possible. But how many of those 350 clients have more money and need extensive individual help?

When was the last time you spoke with your adviser? Did she call you to suggest a change to your retirement plan? Or did he say, "I have a new opportunity that's a lot better than what you have now." Be aware. Your adviser is attempting to cash in on a new commission or transfer fee. This expensive game is played all the time and is perfectly legal. If the last product he sold you is no good now, why does he say this new annuity, stock or mutual fund is better and for how long? Jumping around from product to product is costly— you might as well be day-trading. Hiring a genuine fee-only fiduciary with your interests and understanding of the investing process with a long-term plan avoids this nasty game.

As an investor, you pay for all the middlemen, floor clerks, and telecommunications and other electronic apparatus that make markets run smoothly.
—Arthur Levitt, former SEC Secretary.

Seventy percent of participants in Employer retirement plans believe their plan is free.
—Phyllis Borzi

Management Costs

Dan recalls the moment when he discovered how much we were paying for our tech funds. The Morningstar.com "portfolio" feature reports expenses of each investment along with a total cost for all holdings. We were paying about $16,500 in annual expenses at the height of our portfolio in 2000 (1.1% fees X $1.5 million). Dan recoiled. We never anticipated so much money went to fees even with so-called no load funds. Dan wanted to keep the money in our account, not in some manager's pocket. Of course, those fees were transparent and upfront but for us amateur investors it was startling.

After the dot com disaster, we began a voracious pursuit of lower costs. Figure 40 compares our current average annual costs (.35%) with three other cost structures. We calculated an estimate of our investment costs from 2004 through 2011 to see how we fared with our new lower costs. The results pleased us. The previous $16,500 average per year is now about $5,283 which is reasonable given the size of our portfolio.

The left bar (of the four) represents the highest cost—three percent. This rate is *not* an uncommon expense. Sad to say, many investors pay more than three percent for retail brokerage services. An investor with a 1.5 million dollar portfolio may easily pay $45,000 in costs to a brokerage firm and probably *not know it*. The power of compounding disappears. It is gone...kaput.

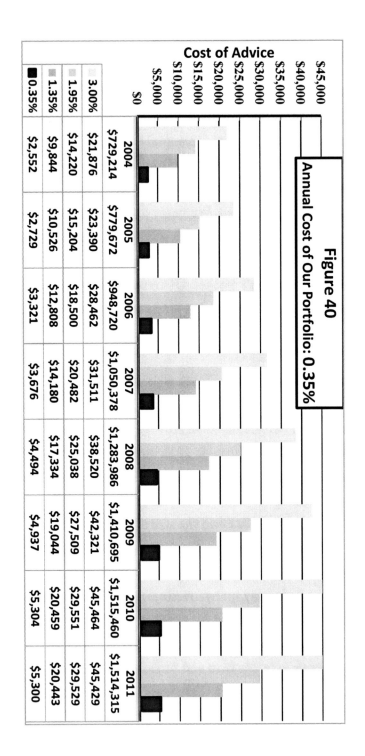

Figure 40

Annual Cost of Our Portfolio: 0.35%

Cost of Advice	2004	2005	2006	2007	2008	2009	2010	2011
3.00%	$729,214	$779,672	$948,720	$1,050,378	$1,283,986	$1,410,695	$1,515,460	$1,514,315
1.95%	$21,876	$23,390	$28,462	$31,511	$38,520	$42,321	$45,464	$45,429
1.35%	$14,220	$15,204	$18,500	$20,482	$25,038	$27,509	$29,551	$29,529
0.35%	$9,844	$10,526	$12,808	$14,180	$17,334	$19,044	$20,459	$20,443
■ 0.35%	$2,552	$2,729	$3,321	$3,676	$4,494	$4,937	$5,304	$5,300

The second bar from the left shows a 1.95 percent fee. The 1 percent financial adviser's Assets Under Management (AUM of 1% is a frequent rate) expense is added the industry average expense (1 percent plus .95 percent =1.95 percent). We calculated a conservative .95 percent cost, lower than the M* industry average fee. It's not necessary to exaggerate costs. Even with our conservative cost estimates the resulting data are clear—they're astronomical!

The second bar from the right represents the 1.35 percent paid by an investor who has a low cost portfolio resembling ours. The investor pays an additional one percent for AUM to an adviser. We added one percent to .35 percent for the 1.35 percent cost.

As you can see the differences are huge—the one percent cost of hiring an adviser to monitor a portfolio like ours is the price for pseudo peace of mind. A second option would work more in your favor: hire a fee-only financial adviser and get genuine peace of mind and perhaps a better return.

Knowing how you pay your financial adviser (fee-only vs. AUM), what type of service they provide (review objective information on Table 13 and costs in Appendix D), and knowing how their investing philosophy fits yours (passive vs. active) is more important than locating the perfect investment. This professional relationship is so important we wrote this chapter and the next to address finding and working with fiduciary advisers.

Value Added or Sales Pitch?

Active managers and advisers will claim to add value as a justification for their fees. Don't believe it— it's a sales pitch. The next time your financial adviser calls to recommend transfers you don't understand, you've been forewarned. Many advisers might suggest now is "the time to buy Apple stock currently at $595 a share because it is going to $800 a share."

Does this Apple stock purchase fit your established plan? What is the commission? What happens when Apple hits $800 and everybody says it's going to $900? What will you do? What are the capital gains taxes if sold at $800 and then what will you buy next? What if the stock decreases in value? At what point do you sell? What do you buy next with the proceeds? If these questions can't be answered, fire this adviser. You are taking excessive risk and paying too much for sales pitches and besides, stay the heck away from individual stocks.

By the way, there is nothing wrong with owning Apple Stock. We own about $5,250 in Apple stock. You now know the *Total Stock Market Index* holds Apple stock. Apple Stock capitalization represents 3.5 percent of the index.

We hold about $150,000 in Vanguard's Total Stock Market Index alone. A simple calculation of *3.5 percent X $150,000 = $5,250.* Apple stock is less risky in the index than owning individual Apple stock shares. Furthermore, if the stock goes up, we still profit. If it tanks, it's not a problem because of diversification.

Fee-Only Adviser

What is the primary advantage of paying a fee-only adviser? The fixed fee agreement reduces hideous conflicts of interest. With our knowledge of avoiding product-driven and actively managed mutual funds we are in the sweet spot to skip or avoid those annual fees and costs discussed. Our adviser charges by the hour and assists us in setting up our plan with low-cost index funds and helps us stick with it during stock market volatility. This adviser wouldn't suggest you buy apple stock.

Charges vary, up to several hundred dollars per hour. Depending on your needs, some may want to charge you a percentage of your assets. Before you decide to pay any adviser by AUM, review Figure 40 above. In our opinion, a fixed fee for advice is much cheaper than paying AUM.

We are getting closer to locating our financial adviser who looks out for us. From the discussion of Table 13 we know the differences between sales pitches, objective information and the fee data. Our search is much easier if we know in advance, in a general way, what we want from our adviser.

After we verify our potential fee-only adviser has a clean record obtained by the National Association of Securities Dealers website (NASD.org), possesses a CFA or RIA certification mentioned early in the chapter and is a member of the National Association of Personal Financial Advisors at *www.napfa.org*, we're almost there. NAPFA can help you find a fee-only financial planner in your area—members of NAPFA are required to sign a fiduciary oath (See Appendix E). Take a copy of this oath to your adviser and ask him or her to sign it.

In working with a fee-only adviser we will use the information learned here and evaluate your adviser's recommendations. The adviser is an important supporter to help adhere to your original plan. A fiduciary has no financial incentive to recommend expensive products without your knowledge. Doing so makes her liable since it's against the fiduciary agreement.

Will You Sign A Check for Advice?

Some financial professionals insist few people will write a check for fee-only advice. This cultural reluctance is a costly mistake—we think nothing of paying for other professional services—mechanic, tax preparer or dental hygienist. Have you heard complaints about writing a check for a rodent exterminator, chimney-sweep or a bookie? Yet, when it comes to paying out of pocket for financial advice we are told people balk.

An initial expense of a few hundred dollars for a fiduciary fee-only adviser *increases* the portfolio gains by one third over time. We encourage you to join the financial "counterculture" and write a check for genuine fiduciary's advice.

The Missing Fiduciary: You

Once in a while an astute investor still gets taken. One of Steve's teacher colleagues hired a fee-only adviser. She paid this crook $200 an hour and he put her in a loaded mutual fund. If she had verified his qualifications with NAPFA and his recommendations she would have recognized on the spot this adviser was a scumbag and left.

Unfortunately for Steve's colleague, she needed a few more of the basics without assuming all fee only advisers are trustworthy. Trust is not part of the equation, but being proactive on your side of this relationship is. Specifically she hadn't asked for the signed fiduciary statement which specifies the adviser will not sell funds paying commissions or revenue sharing costs. She also neglected to look up the tickers on Yahoo. It's up to us as savvy consumers to verify our financial adviser looks out for our best interests. This case is solved—*you* are the ultimate fiduciary.

Assuming you and the potential adviser have similar investing philosophies (index or passive strategy) you can follow-up on each recommended fund using the ticker symbol. Just insert the ticker symbols in Yahoo finance to ascertain the funds that don't charge commissions or have high expense ratios. If the adviser's recommendations have loads you don't want, the fiduciary standards set by

NAPFA have been violated.

You can avoid conflicts, save time (and money) by bringing a lazy portfolio type plan to the first meeting. You are interviewing the adviser to see if their philosophy fits yours. After exchanging pleasantries show the adviser the lazy portfolio and ask him or her to help with *your* portfolio choices. You'll find out in five minutes if the adviser meets your investment philosophy with low cost investments. If you feel like you're getting the run-around, leave. It's simple. But we believe most advisers will work with you—they are real people who want to help. You can't fail as you have educated yourself and studied chapter nine. You have chosen low-cost investments and are in an excellent position to ask for the fiduciary's oath in writing and negotiate the fee.

If you know these basics of working with a fee-only adviser you are ready. You don't have to be reticent— you know so much more than we did 20 years ago. Steve didn't even know a TSA was a 403(b) until he was 45 years old. Dan didn't know about mutual funds until he was 48. Neither of us knew how to diversify our holdings with low-cost funds and rebalance for another decade.

You know what appropriate long-term investments versus product-driven advice and inappropriate retirement products look like. You know different fee structures and the effects of those costs over time. You know enough to locate an ethical adviser and monitor their services much better than we did when we were sold five annuities. And finally, you know what objective financial information looks like versus sales pitches. What are you waiting for?

Still not sure? Here is a simple exam. *One of the following financial advisers' comments reflects a genuine fee-only fiduciary:*

1. "My fees are paid by the interest earned on your account and not from your principle."

2. "This complimentary session is to see if we are a match. My job is to help you set up a diversified portfolio, keep it diversified and support you. If you decide to hire me, my fee is $200 per hour in face-to-face meetings."

3. "With the help of our research department I can tell which of your funds aren't doing well, and re-invest the money in more 'profitable' investments."

The responsible genuine fee-only fiduciary answer is at the beginning of the next chapter.

Steve Schullo and Dan Robertson

Answer to previous chapter question: 2

Why are the other two comments incorrect?
1. Is a thinly veiled sales pitch expertly designed to trick you into thinking that interest is not as important as your principle. Compounded interest (or yield) is your money too!
3. Is a sophisticated sales pitch to forecast returns. No person **or** their complicated formulae can predict the future.

CHAPTER 12

A Conversation with a Fee-Only Fiduciary

The best financial advisers, I've found after a year of listening to them, are thoughtful and pragmatic, don't take themselves too seriously, and are confident enough in their knowledge that they need not hyperventilate when issuing advice.

Numbers by Lee Eisenberg

Prologue: Let's eavesdrop on a fictional conversation between a client and a **genuine** fiduciary financial adviser. Samantha, a 30- year-old client, needs assistance with her employer sponsored retirement plan. Using the objective information on the right columns of Table 13 in chapter 11, we created the following "conversation."

SETTING: FINANCIAL ADVISER'S OFFICE.

Adviser: "I've reviewed your background information about your retirement plan. Thanks for sending it to me.

This is a complimentary meeting to see if we are a good fit, so let's get started. How did you hear about me?"

Samantha: "Ben, my fiancé, encouraged me to see an adviser. My great friends, Carolyn and her partner Madison, have you for their adviser. Both recommended you without hesitation. Carolyn has experienced several advisers and trusts you the most."

Adviser: "Yes, of course. They're a wonderful couple and great people. I'm flattered. They work hard to learn how to manage their investments. They are my most knowledgeable clients—as I'll point out in a few minutes, that's an important part of our professional relationship. Tell me more about your investments."

Samantha: "I started saving for retirement through work several years ago. First, I bought my company stock and then I went into a safer investment when the stock went down in 2008. I read a little about investing but it seemed complicated. Ben and I went to investment lunches but I felt like they were trying to railroad me. Ben didn't like the insurance products either. So, he decided to invest on his own. He showed me what he was doing, but neither one of us knew enough about my 401(k) plan.

When I told him I was thinking about seeing an adviser, he encouraged me, but told me to avoid the freebie financial advisers. 'When you pay somebody by the hour, you'll get honest advice,' he said."

Adviser: "It's good to have support at home and from good friends. Many couples don't talk about money.

How can I help?"

Samantha: "I'm not sure. My folks said my money might not be spread out enough" (She shows the adviser her financial spreadsheet).

Adviser: "Thanks, I looked at this in the email you sent me. Let's see, you have $35,000 in a 401(k) plan and you work in the IT department as your company's web master. You own a condo with a mortgage of about $120,000, with a $1,300 per month payment. Your car is paid for and you have no other debts. Sounds very good. What's the 401(k) money for?"

Samantha: "It's for retirement. I plan not to touch it."

Adviser: "Do you have a retirement age in mind?"

Samantha: "Yes, at about 60, another 30 years. This may change when my future husband gets involved with both our finances. But for now, let's say 60."

Adviser: "You have a great start, particularly the actions you've already taken in learning to start a solid plan and knowing when to ask for help. (Looks at the spreadsheet.) You have $28,000 in your 401(k) in a Stable Value fund and $7000 in Flat Tire Company (FTC) stock, where you work."

Samantha: "Thanks for pointing that out. I know enough to have both bonds and stocks and that's what I have. But I don't know what kind of bonds or stocks to invest in."

Adviser: "You're correct about having both, but it's not diversified enough. You have 80 percent of your retirement plan in the stable value fund. Do you know what a stable value fund is?"

Samantha: "I think so. It doesn't lose money, like a bank savings account. That's why I chose it. My company's stock lost money four years ago when the market tanked. I asked the Human Resources department if I could sell it. They said I couldn't."

Adviser: "Why?"

Samantha: "I don't remember. The person I spoke to tried to tell me the stock price goes up and down. I was confused and really bothered. He suggested I put my next retirement deductions into an account that doesn't lose money. I started contributing into the stable value fund and stopped buying the stock. I have serious doubts about buying real stocks."

Adviser: "Your stable value fund is also called a fixed account but 80 percent is too much for a young investor because it won't grow much. It's fine to have some of your money in this account since you kept contributing even during the 2008 crash. Lots of people stopped altogether. Is there anything else you would like to tell me before we continue?"

Samantha: "No that's about it. What should I do?"

Adviser: "First, you need to find out about your company's retirement plan policy, the investment choices and why you couldn't sell the stock. Second, if we decide to meet again, we can make changes. Your problem of spreading out, diversifying, is easy to fix because you are now a regular saver. For most people that's the hardest part. Diversification means finding the best mix of stocks and bonds through mutual funds. Most people come here knowing *nothing* about their current retirement plan and want me to fix and manage it 100 percent. It costs more, but after learning a few basics you can save a lot of money. You've already started to learn, so you're in a better position to tell me your direction and this helps me to help you."

Samantha: (relieved). "Oh, thanks, I was a little nervous because I didn't think I knew enough. I should know more."

Adviser: "Of course. I encourage my clients to know as much as they can about investing. I'll give you a short reading list to get started. It's your money and only you can take the responsibility for your retirement. My job is to help you learn which investments are available on your employer's 401(k) plan which will work best for you. This will get clearer as we go along. We'll work on a plan with some risk to grow and preserves what you have earned. It's a delicate balancing act to help you prepare for down markets.

It is surprising how a little financial self-education on investing help clients sleep through market fluctuations."

Samantha: "I know the feeling. I freaked four years ago when my FTC stock went down."

Adviser: "Find out why you couldn't sell. What are the restrictions? Who is the administrator and record keeper? Usually companies farm this out to one of the large mutual fund companies. There must be a brochure or information online. I could look it up for you, but that would take more time. I want you to do this. OK?"

Samantha: "Yes, I'll find out. Oh yeah, I remember getting a 15 percent discount on FTC stock."

Adviser: "Sounds like a good deal. Ask your HR department for the company's list of investments in your company's 401(k) and most importantly, the costs. Be sure to include the ticker symbol, it's a five-letter identification of each mutual fund. Your 401(k) plan should have a list of mutual funds." (Samantha is writing down her list of needed information.)

"As I was saying, I'll offer recommendations you'll understand to get you to your retirement goal."

Samantha: "OK, that sounds fair. My fiancé suggested I ask you if you're… ah, I forget the word, it's something about looking after my interests…"

Adviser: "Your fiancé is on the ball. He wants to know if I am a fiduciary."

Samantha: "Yes. Now I remember, do you sign fiduciary agreements with your clients."

Adviser: "Here it is."

Samantha: "That *was* quick. I owe Ben a dinner, thanks."

Adviser: "First, let me explain this agreement, it is the basis of our professional relationship should you hire me. As your fiduciary, I will *not* put you in funds which pay me commissions. I work strictly on an hourly basis. Together we pick the funds which meet your best interests. Your investments are not paying me, you are. When you hire a contractor, mechanic or a CPA, they charge a onetime fee. I work the same way. If you want to hire me, my fee is $200 per hour and there are no other fees. But what I want is that you be willing to learn to take responsibility for your plan."

Samantha: "I like the direction we are going. You removed the inherent complications about your fee as Ben wanted. It's very straightforward. But I'm not sure how I can take responsibility for my plan."

Adviser: "That's why I get paid. It's training you, in a sense, about becoming empowered to take charge. Honestly, Samantha, I think you can do this. Believe me, $200 per hour is cheaper than paying a percentage of your portfolio. Most important, you'll feel confident knowing you have an understandable plan. While I will never promise which stock or mutual fund will outperform the market, I can promise you will know how to begin to take responsibility after our next session and in the future. It's a gradual process. OK?"

Samantha: "I appreciate your incremental approach, the explanation about fees, how you are compensated and the risk of FTC stock. You answered my initial question about diversification. I didn't know this. As I said, I like where we are going. Alright, let's go for it. I'll fax the information about my employer's options as soon as I find out. Let's make an appointment now."

Adviser: "Great. Just stop by my secretary's desk."

Two Days Later

SETTING: FLAT TIRE COMPANY'S

HUMAN RESOURCE DEPARTMENT

Samantha: "Good morning. I have a 401(k) account and would like to know more about the plan."

Clerk: "Here is a brochure showing the company's plan."

Samantha: (Looking at the brochure). "Thanks, I see the list of mutual funds but I don't see the costs."

Clerk: "That's all I have. Here is the phone number to get more information."

Samantha: "Before I call this number, just wanted to let you know I am seeing a financial adviser. She asked me to get the costs. It's important."

Clerk: "Let me ask my supervisor, excuse me."

Supervisor: "Good morning, may I help you?"

Samantha: "I have the brochure listing my choices for my 401(k) plan. I am seeing a financial adviser and she is requesting the costs of each choice. It doesn't say here."

Supervisor: "If you have a 401(k) plan with us, you can find information in your account online. Also, if you want to talk to a person you'll find a phone number on the brochure. Flat Tire Company contracts with an outside investment firm to help you with the 401(k) plan. Our company pays the fees for record keeping and administration at no cost to you. Each fund has its own expense, which you need to ask for."

Samantha: "Great!"

Supervisor: "This is not the usual question employees ask. I know FTC contracts with Fidelity Investments; here is their number."

Samantha: "Do we have retirement planning workshops for employees?"

Supervisor: "Yes, I was going to mention this. The next one is in two weeks. They are scheduled on the first

Wednesday every three months. They'll talk about all of your benefits: pension plan, medical, dental and retirement plans. It's located in the employee lounge. They will answer all of your questions. From what I have heard, employees like the information presented."

Samantha: "Great, thank you. Do I have to register?"

Supervisor: "No, it's informal, just show up. Watch for the notice in the employee lounge."

Samantha: "Thank you."

Later that day

ON THE PHONE TO XYZ CONSULTANTS

Samantha: "Hi, I'm trying to get information about my 401(k) plan. I'm working with a financial adviser and she wants to know the costs for the different choices."

XYZ Consultant: "You can get this information online by logging on with your social security number and employee number. Are you in front of a computer?"

Samantha: "No, not now, but I will be later. I want to talk to you first (looking at her notes from her conversation with her adviser). My adviser wants to see FTC's list of choices. I have the 401(k) list, but it doesn't say what the costs are."

XYZ Consultant: "FTC pays the costs for their employees and offers a 6 percent match. The company has been very happy with our services."

Samantha: "I agree. FTC is a good company. Do you have the list of funds I can use in my 401(k)?"

XYZ Consultant confirms the following list with Samantha:

1. Life Cycle Funds from TR Price 2015-2050
2. Stable Value
3. Long-term Bond Index
4. Extended Market Index
5. S&P 500 Index
6. Growth Stock Index
7. Value Stock Index
8. Growth Stock Fund
9. Small Cap Index
10. International Stock Index
11. International Stock Fund

Samantha: "Great, but it doesn't have the costs."

XYZ Consultant: "There are no costs because FTC pays the record keeping and the administrative costs. It's in the contract between our financial firm and the company. Sorry, I am not privy to the information in the contract."

Samantha: OK, it's just my adviser wants to know what the costs are. She made it sound like there has to be costs."

XYZ Consultant: "Of course, there are costs but as I have already said, you can tell your adviser there are no costs. This is a common agreement with 401(k) plans."

Samantha: "Alright, I'll take your word. I have two more questions. What are the ticker symbols?"

XYZ Consultant: "These funds are for the exclusive use of FTC employees, so most do not have ticker symbols, except for these three: Balanced fund is VWELX, Extended Market is VEXMX and the International fund is HANIX."

Samantha: "Great, my adviser can find out the costs of those three with ticker symbols. Can I sell my FTC stock?"

XYZ Consultant: "Yes, after you have owned it for a year."

Samantha: "Good, I have owned it for four years. My adviser recommends I sell some to diversify into a mutual fund. I have about 20 percent of my portfolio in the stock."

XYZ Consultant: "Which fund would you like to trade your stock to?"

Samantha: "I don't know. I'll talk to my adviser first. Alright, it looks like I have all of the information I need. We'll come up with a plan and I'll call back with my decision. Thanks."

SECOND APPOINTMENT WITH ADVISER

Adviser: "You've done your homework. I'm impressed! How'd it go?"

Samantha: "I was anxious. I think this one guy got irritated because I kept asking about costs. Two different people assured me the company pays for the costs. I also learned about my other benefits. I didn't know I had a pension too."

Adviser: "Good. Later on I want to know about your pension benefits for your long term retirement goals. But let's stay with what you have to do right now. I'm looking at your company's 401(k) plan on this website,

Brightscope.com. It evaluates plans for thousands of companies. Take a look on my computer. They rated your 401(k) 77, an above average score. Fees are 1.64 percent. It's high, but fortunately for you, your company pays for this."

Samantha: "The clerk said people never ask about fees."

Adviser: "It's strange. But he is right, people usually don't ask about costs even though they do with *everything else* in life. Let's move on. We've a lot to cover today. We want to diversify."

Samantha: "Yes. I am free to sell all of my shares."

Adviser: "Do you want to start your stock option plan again? I think it's a good idea to take advantage of the 15 percent discount."

Samantha: "I'm not sure. Can I wait?"

Adviser: "Of course."

Samantha: "Shall I sell all of my stock?"

Adviser: "Yes, if you are comfortable. As you know, there are no tax consequences in the tax deferred plan."

Samantha: "Can I do half?"

Adviser: "Yes. An excellent start. You have enough money to construct a portfolio and diversify into some of the *asset classes*. Do you know about asset classes?"

Samantha: "No."

Adviser: "Asset classes are the "core" stocks which most portfolios should have. You want to know where the proceeds of the FTC stock are going to set up a diversified portfolio. These core classes are called large-cap company, intermediate-cap, small-cap, international and bond funds. There are large and small-cap internationals too, which we'll discuss next year. All portfolios should have these core classes. They provide growth and stability. Are you following me?"

Samantha: "What does 'cap' mean?'

Adviser: "Cap is short for capitalization. The size of the company is determined by their capitalization, their number of shares times the price of the stock. Apple and Exxon are the two biggest companies because their total share value is the highest of all 500 corporations here in the United States offering stock to the public. The familiar name for this group of large-cap companies is the Standard and Poor's, or the S&P 500 index. So you see how diversification is set up with these 500 large-cap companies in one fund. Neat, huh?"

Samantha: "Yes, I hear about the S&P 500 in the news."

Adviser: "The S&P 500 index is *one* core holding. The other two are mid-cap and small-cap. You are lucky the Extended Market index is available (VEXMX). It's from Vanguard and it only charges .28%."

Samantha: "How did you know?"

Adviser: "I already knew this ticker symbol, but if I didn't I can do a Google search with the ticker symbol V-E-X-M-X. It will take me to the fund company website offering this fund and I can find out all the information I need to get started. But we're lucky—I already know this excellent index fund."

Samantha: "That's why you asked me to get the ticker symbol. I have a funny feeling you like this fund" (smiling).

Adviser: "You are very lucky this fund is available to you. It has medium size companies and small size companies in the same fund. Your company plan has the S&P 500 index and the Extended Market index available. With these two funds, you own a piece of all of the domestic companies. These are good to start with. As your portfolio grows you'll eventually invest in several asset classes outside the United States, for example, with an international fund for broader exposure. You already have a fixed account in 'stable value'. By the way, $35,000 is not chump change. Very few 30-year-olds have so much put away for retirement and have no credit card debt!"

 Samantha: "My parents pushed me to save even as a child and we're all pleased how savings add up. Aren't foreign company's risky investments?"

Adviser: "Yes, they are and so are American companies. All investments have risk. Let's talk about risk. The books on the list I gave you talk about risk. Here is a short course: Most people understand the basic premise of diversifying investments – the idea not to put all your eggs in one basket. But they don't know how and they sometimes think diversification eliminates risk. Diversification helps manage risk; it can't eliminate it. One end of risk is doing nothing with your money; putting it under your mattress. In a sense stable value is safe but it doesn't earn enough to keep up with inflation. The other extreme is to bet it all at craps in Vegas. It might work but more likely will cost you everything. Proper investment risk consists of finding a balanced middle ground between growth potential and protection from down markets. A single stock, even your FTC stock, is unpredictable which is why we recommend funds.

With 20 percent of your money in FTC stock you probably know what I am going to say—you're taking a big risk over the long term. And yet with a 15 percent discount a short-term risk is worth the risk. After a year, sell the stock and reinvest the money into a broadly diversified index fund.

Flat Tire Company is a large-cap company, so it's in the S&P 500. Its total stock value is $60 billion. Remember, you still own FTC stock in the S&P 500 with 499 other companies too."

Samantha: "I thought that's what you'd say about my FTC stock, after you talked about being diversified in different companies. Interesting, FTC went down and then it came back just as my work colleague said it would."

Adviser: "What if it didn't recover, like Enron or WorldCom the long distance phone company? Those unfortunate employees thought the same thing about their company and they lost all of their savings. Of course, it's the worst case scenario. The volatility alone about investing in one company is not a good thing for long-term growth. Look, it's fine to invest in FTC stock, but 4 percent of your holding is reasonable and less risky.

Remember how you felt when it first went down? You

stopped buying. That was scary."

Samantha: "Do I remember! After what I have been through with my company stock in 2008, I get it!"

Adviser: "Great. Does the company offer a match to the 401(k) plan?"

Samantha: "Six percent."

Adviser: "Smart move, you realize it's free money. How are we doing?"

Samantha: "When I came here I wondered if I would trust you with my money, like, what would you recommend and would the investments be good for me. But that's not what you have said at all. You are not recommending individual stocks, you're recommending I invest in all available companies. It's information I didn't expect. You have reversed the decisions and put the responsibility right back on me. The most convincing part is your recommendation of the broad asset classes which invest in all companies. Furthermore, you showed me how I can take responsibility and make the decisions. Not necessarily the right or wrong decision to invest in this or that particular investment but to decide to invest in *all companies.* I believe I understand where we are going and I am getting more comfortable. I get it about moving my money from owning individual FTC stock to an index reduces risk.

Adviser: "Yes, the point is to stick with a plan you set up and *understand.* The biggest mistake people make is trusting somebody else 100 percent with their money, paying too much for advice, not knowing enough about diversification and taking on too much risk. People may not admit it but they look for the one or two investments to get to their financial goals quickly."

Samantha: "Yes, I like the slow and grow approach. OK, it looks to me like the S&P 500 and the Extended Stock Index will be a good start. I am investing in all available companies in the United States, and with the FTC's 6 percent match in my 401(k) plan."

Adviser: "It's simple and straightforward. Index funds are a much better strategy for managing risk than actively managed funds because actively managed funds cost more and they take on more risk. You don't need more risk. Because of lower costs the indexes outperform managed funds seventy to eighty percent of the time according to many academic studies. By staying with the indexed fund, you are passive in the sense you are not trading based on media hype or fears."

Samantha: "Don't managers also invest in the same asset classes?"

Adviser: "Usually not. They buy and sell trying to beat what you would have gotten if you just stayed invested in the entire asset class and be done with it. For example, I recommend the S&P 500 index from the list. You would be investing in the largest corporations in the United States. It's an appropriate investment to start."

Samantha: "Ben talks about buying and selling stocks, like the active managers. Is he doing something wrong?"

Adviser: "Well, his strategy is *not* the strategy we are talking about. I think you don't want to buy and sell stocks."

Samantha: "You are absolutely right. I hate it, even though I love my company. And the more I hear you talk about the indexes compared to trading stocks, the more I like passive strategy. It feels natural to me somehow."

Adviser: "That's because a study reports that women are better long-term investors than men. As we have been saying about long-term thinking, men are more likely to jump in and out of investments in the short-term whereas women think long-term and stick with the same investments. Guess what? Women's investment returns are higher, duh."

Samantha: "Really? How funny. Wait till I tell Ben, my mom and my dad (laughing)."

Adviser: "What is equally interesting is that women are not any smarter investors than men. Women stay with their investments longer, avoiding all of the costs associated with trading, buying high and selling low. That's all."

Samantha: "Thanks for telling me that. I thought I had to trade to be a successful investor. This is reassuring."

Adviser: "Other people think advisers can pick winners. We can't! I don't know the next hot stock. Warren Buffett says he doesn't know either. But people are funny. They think just because someone has financial training, a certificate, a practice and a computer, they can find the next stock to make them rich (also laughing).

"My philosophy is long-term, slow growth, low costs, and broad diversification with rebalancing. Slowly grow your portfolio until you retire. For you, that's in 30 years. My job is to help you stay the course, stick to your plan, over good times and bad. I am your support when the market acts up and that's when your trust in me will be challenged. You know, when your stock went down 30 percent four years ago, I would have said the same thing your work colleague said: 'Don't sell, it's going to be OK.'"

Samantha: "Sounds like you offer more than just a strategy and information, but psychological support too?"

Adviser: "I am not a psychologist. But yes, that's precisely how I can assist you, after you set up a plan today. I will not leave you alone. Just one step at a time. One of the books I recommend is a book on psychology called *Your Money and Your Mind* by Jason Zweig.

"When it comes to losing money people get irrational. People think they have good sense but most overreact with terrible consequences. It's a normal response to freak out, but disastrous for your long term plan. But you couldn't sell and it bounced back. That emotional experience *cannot be taught*. The next time a loss happens you won't be so upset. You might feel bad in the short term and wonder where your adviser, me, is leading you but you're less vulnerable to panic selling."

Samantha: "The indexing strategy, low costs and all, doesn't get rid of my worrying about losing money, does it? But I am relieved that you told me now that my trust in you might be tested when the market goes down. You really know your business. You can predict people's emotions ahead of time, but not the market. Interesting."

Adviser: "But you also know that no strategy can eliminate risk and that information should relieve you also. The indexing strategy reduces risk. Diversification, education and thinking long term have a better chance of protecting you from losing sleep. Steep losses are short-term and are almost always due to poor diversification. Your reading homework talks about managing risk which will reduce your worry and resulting irrational decision making."

Samantha: "The investment book I read didn't say anything about indexing. When the market goes down, the index goes down too, right?"

Adviser: "Yes it does. Most books don't talk about indexing. The books I've compiled for clients follow John Bogle's strategy. The easiest way to think about index funds is to visualize the index fund's relationship to the broad economy -- companies, services, people working, companies growing. Think about the 5000 or so companies in Fidelity's or Vanguard's Total Stock Market Index representing our economy. An index fund invests in all of the available companies. The economy grows because the companies grow and so will the indexes because they *follow* the broad economy—the companies and the economy are one. You only have to trust the broad economy across the entire planet will continue to *grow* over the years.

In contrast, active mutual fund managers and stockbrokers want to make more than what the economy can provide. Sometimes they get lucky and pick the fastest growing part of the economy, like technology during the bubble in the late 1990s, but then fail to pick the next part or sector. That inconsistency is unproductive and extremely costly. Dalbar, a respected research firm, reports from 1991 through 2010 the S&P 500 20-year average was 9.14 percent, while the average mutual fund investor earned 3.83 percent."

Samantha: "Wow! That's a big difference. Why do so many investors fail?"

Adviser: "Like we discussed, they jump in and out of the stocks or funds, buy high and then sell them low when they get scared and into a fixed account to stop the bleeding. In addition they pay capital gains taxes, trading costs, front-end and back-end commissions. In an index, none of those fees apply and the index returns what the broad economy returned over those years."

Samantha: "Your explanation of what investors do wrong makes sense. I didn't understand what you meant when you first said experiencing stock market volatility is not easily taught, but now I do. My stock has recovered and went higher after the 2008 crash. I think I made money on my stock because I bought some stocks when it went down. I should have kept buying when the shares cost less. But everybody was selling, except my one colleague. I am beginning to understand about long-term thinking and how risk can work for me, not against me."

Adviser: "Exactly. And you heard your colleague say to you, 'Don't worry, the stock will recover.' Most people would have thought her a fool for hanging on to a losing stock."

Samantha: "I feel good about our conversation. When I first called for an appointment, I had never thought about this. I forgot why I came here because I am learning so much now. I'm smart, but finances, money and investing were those things somebody else understood. But you kept explaining the big picture. When you said only I can take the responsibility, I thought *what the heck am I paying you for?* But you're right. I'm still a little foggy on the details but the major idea is investing may not be as complicated and intimidating as I thought it was. Investing in the broad economies did it for me. Thanks."

Adviser: "Besides experiencing risk and volatility, thinking long-term is difficult for most people. You understand this and you are on your way to managing a responsible retirement plan."

Samantha: "Well, I'll have to take your word."

Adviser: "No you don't. People look at their investments at the moment of a market crash and just don't see better days ahead. Or they didn't anticipate market declines by allocating enough in bonds during bull markets. In other words, *they didn't have a plan.* You're fortunate. You understand risk, volatility and thinking long-term by having a plan."

Samantha: "I think I got it. I feel comfortable transferring half of the $28,000 into the Extended Market Index. I'm glad there are no taxes because it is tax-deferred. And I'll have a plan to help me understand and keep on track."

Adviser: "Great. We've achieved a lot today. Let's write up your plan. You know how to make those changes. I'll recommend just two changes to jump-start your plan. Always remember we're planning for the *long term* and we'll make additional changes later as you contribute more money. Sorry for the mini-lecture, but this is the first step and will diversify your current holdings. OK?"

Samantha: "It's a deal and you're not lecturing. I need to hear this. Show me what I need to do. I can handle two changes and see how it goes, although I am a little nervous."

Adviser: "Change is always difficult, but after you see your plan, you will be more comfortable. You have $35,000 total: $7,000 in stock plus $28,000 in the stable value. I recommend you sell half of the stock holding and invest it in the S&P 500 index. I would take half of the Stable Value fund and put it into Extended Market Index, $14,000. These two moves give you your first diversified core holdings.

Your monthly contribution continues to go to Stable Value. We'll wait for about a year and when you're comfortable again, we can move to Phase II. Next year you put the rest of your FTC holdings into the S&P 500 and move $14,000 from Stable Value into the International Index. How does that sound?"

Samantha: "Perfect."

Samantha's Current Portfolio

FTC Stock: $7,014.07 (20% of Portfolio, 77.77 Shares@$90.19)

Stable Value: $28,000.00 (80% of the Portfolio, earning 3%)

After today's changes,
SAMANTHA's portfolio will look like this
Phase 1

FTC Stock	$3,500	10% of total holdings
S&P 500 Index	$3,500	10% of total holdings
Stable Value (fixed account)	$14,000	40% of total holdings
Extended Market Index (VEXMX)	$14,000	40% of total holdings
Total	**$35,000**	**100% of holdings**

Next Year
(All account figures are estimates.
Future portfolio growth is unknown)
Phase 2

FTC Stock	$0.00 (Remaining shares will be sold and transferred to the S&P 500 Index [Will decide about purchasing more stock via the stock option plan.])
S&P 500 Index	$7,000 (15% of Portfolio, from FTC Stock account).
Stable Value (fixed account)	$10,000 (22% of Portfolio, estimated contributions for the next 12 months). Will decide to either continue contributions or buy directly to the International Stock Index account.
Extended Market Index (VEXMX)	$14,000 (31% of Portfolio)
International Stock Index	$14,000 (31% of Portfolio)
Total	**$45,000 (Estimated) 100% of holdings**

Additional Notes from the Adviser:

- Read John Bogle's book to learn about indexing strategy. Log on to the www.boglehead.org investment forum and/or the www.403bwise.com investment forums to ask questions and read what other individual investors are doing.

- Unless something urgent is needed, we will not need my services for a year. In the coming years, we will eventually set up a 70 percent equity/30 percent bond portfolio.

- After the Phase 1 changes, the portfolio has about 60 percent equities and 40 percent fixed securities. This stock/bond split is too conservative for a 30-year-old, but it is an appropriate starting point.

Adviser: "Let me explain your plan. After you make the first two changes, you'll have about 40 percent fixed accounts and 60 percent stocks. Investing in stocks will provide the growth to outpace the negative effects of inflation. The reading material will help explain in detail how and why equities grow more than bonds. Right now you have no international investments. But after your portfolio grows you'll consider them next year. Your portfolio will be diversified enough in phase 1, except you'll still have about 10 percent of your holdings in your company's stock, which will be reallocated next year. This is *your* plan; it's a great plan. You did much of the work. Congratulations Samantha!"

Samantha: "Really? Looked to me like you did most of the work."

Adviser: "OK, I put the pieces together and explained

the big picture. But *you* brought the necessary pieces—*you* requested diversification assistance, *you* experienced stock market volatility, *you* found the mutual funds available from your company's plan, *you* saved $35,000 and *you* took your family's advice by coming here. That's a lot of work and responsibility! What's important is you understand how all of those pieces fit together."

Samantha: "I did all of that? You know, I think this'll work. I have learned a lot. I didn't know diversification meant to invest in not just more stocks, but different types of stocks in different industries, different sizes of companies and other countries. I'd never thought of investing in foreign countries. Now I know how stocks are already diversified in the major asset classes that reflect these differences. I still don't know about rebalancing."

Adviser: "That's because we didn't talk about rebalancing. We will talk about it next year. Show your plan to Ben, your parents, and Carolyn and Madison. How does that sound?"

Samantha: "Great!"

Adviser: "Any final questions?"

Samantha: "No. Not right now. It was a pleasure talking with you. One month ago investing was the last thing on my mind. I was just saving. But now I am thinking about growing my money for the future. Thanks again."

Adviser: "My pleasure. I'll see you in about a year and we'll discuss your progress and phase two."

Authors' Debrief

This conversation demonstrates the guidance of the client toward taking personal responsibility for choices rather than simply steering toward pre-selected advisor's products (funds or annuities).

1. Fee-only Advisement Cost for Samantha: 2.5 hours is $500 out of pocket.

2. If Samantha's money were in an actively managed fund paying the adviser commissions (Load):

   $35000 x 3% commission + 1.25% annual expense ratio =$1050 + 437.50 = $1487.50. As Samantha increases her portfolio, the annual expenses would go up.

3. Investing may not be as complicated, risky or varied as commissioned salespeople would like you to believe. If they can convince you they are financial shamans, there to relieve you of all losses with riskless fixed accounts, rest assured, they will relieve you of the full market returns you deserve.

4. A genuine fiduciary will never enter into any real or potential conflicts of interest when recommending investments to clients and *will never make changes to your plan without your knowledge.*

5. Notice, nowhere in this hypothetical conversation did Samantha and the adviser drift into topics which would not help Samantha's need to understand her plan, the investing process and taking responsibility. For examples, the future of interest rates, China, politics, past, present and future market conditions, gold, real estate, sector funds, futures, options, annuities, the future of the Euro, Greek debt crisis, or—heaven forbid—

looking on the computer screen as the adviser scrolls down the hundreds of different mutual funds to decide where to invest based on past 1-3-5 year performance. These extraneous topics are a total waste of Samantha's valuable time and money.

The authors had a brief experience with a broker who scanned mutual funds on his computer. It was miserable looking at the streaming of one mutual fund after another, like a never-ending, slow moving slot machine. No wonder people are frightened with trusting somebody with their money. We rushed out of his office with the energy of a scared yachtsman bailing out his leaking two-master.

Part Four
Are You Ready?

"If you know how to spend
less than you get, you have the
philosopher's stone."

—Ben Franklin

CHAPTER 13

The Philosopher's Stone

Most people live below their means during bad economic times when we collectively cut back spending as we are in this current lingering Great Recession. The trick is to continue to live below one's means when good times return. When that happens, be prepared to increase (or start) your investment and tax-deferred 403(b)/401(k)/457(b)/Roth IRA contribution and continue to pay down debts. We share how we started and stayed motivated for the purpose of reducing our spending.

We met 37 years ago at a group therapy retreat in the beautiful mountains of Big Bear. Prior to our relationship we were involved in various consciousness raising movements prevalent at the time. We enjoyed yoga, transcendental meditation, Eastern philosophy lectures, anti-war protests and holistic influences.

The encounter group movement helped us seek a deeper understanding of ourselves, others and our place in this world. We discovered the idealism of how life could be, achieving our American dream outside of the mainstream values of trusting authority, consumerism, martini-sipping superficiality, suburban isolationism and the older generation's support for the fear-based expensive cold war and the hot Vietnam War. Wouldn't the world benefit by understanding between nations?

Our anti-establishment peers valued back-to-nature foods, recycling, civic and personal responsibility, civil rights along with meditation for inner and world peace. Meanwhile, back on earth we were just another young couple (Dan, 33/Steve, 27) struggling to make ends meet while in school, starting or changing careers like everyone else.

Simplicity, simplicity, simplicity! I say, let your affairs be as two or three, and not a hundred or a thousand; instead of a million, count half dozen, and keep your accounts on your thumb-nail.

—Henry D. Thoreau

Recall from our stories we came from modest financial and educational family backgrounds with no real estate, little savings, no trusts nor financial gifts and minimal knowledge about investing. Our parents were not college educated and far from affluent. We owned a Beetle and a Squareback and some furniture with a few hundred in the bank. Independence and self-reliance were imperative.

Many Americans share these youthful experiences, starting with idealism and little else, and yet attain comfortable, wholesome and secure wealth. We continue to embrace our early counterculture values and are grateful for our roots in those historic upheavals. Some of those values fit seamlessly into living within our means to build our nest egg while looking out for the environment throughout our adult life.

John Bogle, a Closeted Hippie?

We think so. Mr. Bogle reminds us of what we learned in our youth. His gentle approach is music to our ears, rejecting corporate republic values, especially Wall Street's, where unhealthy *individual* competition dominates the discussion. He eschews those winner-take-all and excessive materialistic values.

According to Bogle's biographer, Lewis Braham, "Bogle drove his 1977 Honda Acura for about 15 years until he was no longer able to and gave it to his son Andrew." When Bogle was CEO of Vanguard he never owned or flew in a private jet or first class, he flew coach. The back of the plane lands at the same time as the front. He's an eloquent example of social and financial conservation.

Mr. Bogle wrote in his book, *Enough*, about competition: "Competition is a part of life. But again I ask, competition for what? For test scores rather than learning? For form rather than substance? For prestige rather than virtue? For certainty rather than ambiguity? For following someone else's stars rather than one's own." Powerful words reflect what we strive for and admire. How neat to find a high profile public person of esteemed stature from a profession as far from these values as Albert Schweitzer is from the Kardashians.

In a rare interview on CNBC with two dark-suited Wall Street cronies, Bogle dared suggest a small tax to discourage reckless and speculative trading. Like two crows sitting on a power pole the Wall Street aficionados squawked "Oh no!" in perfect unison. They were upset with Bogle's mere mention of controlling their excessive trading rhetoric.

He stood his ground by preaching with a twinkle in his eye and decades of quiet tested habits, calculated boldness—exuding honesty and candor. He said speculative trading doesn't make a healthy economy, a responsible financial system or robust individual investors. Like acolytes looking up to an enlightened being, we declared, "We love this man."

> *It's not having what you want.*
> *It's wanting what you've got.*
>
> **—Sheryl Crow**

Home-spun Philosophy: Motivated Saving

A money saving attitude is essential for a financially secure retirement. "Who doesn't know that?" some ask. For starters, millions of Americans between

55 and 65 saved an average of $65,000 for retirement. Many more will depend on social security, a pension or be forced to work indefinitely. According to *The Week* news magazine, "more than a third of men ages 65 to 69 hold jobs, as do more than a quarter of women that age." It's unlikely people who don't save will access their retirement dreams. People know it's a good thing to save, but most don't. Why?

Our money saving ideas are common sense. Still we may have a helpful twist or two to share. It starts with small habits. When we started dating we shared one cup of coffee when we dined out. We knew then we were kindred spirits.

Steve turns the water heater off during the desert summer. The dishwasher heats its own water so we haven't gotten beriberi yet. With the community Jacuzzi 104 degrees and an adjacent shower, we get along fine. We go to the gym four days a week and shower there too, bringing the water bill down as well as keep fit to reduce health costs. During the winter we set the water heater at its lowest setting.

It's not hard to make decisions
when you know what your values are.

—**Roy Disney**

Beyond these snippets is a pervasive attitude about conservation. Frugality goes beyond saving and accumulating money to making fewer demands on natural resources and utilities. For example, composting is an easy way to recycle kitchen refuse—our garden vegetables and flowers are happy. If enough people composted the local city municipality could increase the budget for something beneficial such as recreation and parks and reduce the allotment for garbage treatment.

We ratcheted-up the idea of reducing our energy needs by two huge notches. First, we installed 24 solar panels on our house four years ago. It costs only 60 percent of the overall price due to federal, state and energy company rebates. Our energy bills are less than a dollar a month: a sensible choice with 350 sunny days per year. Not only have we reduced our energy bills, our solar meter reports 52,700 pounds of CO_2 didn't pour into the atmosphere. We were delighted when two of our neighbors followed suit.

Second, we bought a Leaf. The 100 percent electric car replaced Steve's 15-year-old Explorer. It's another opportunity to reduce energy costs. We save on electric bills and won't be purchasing expensive and polluting petroleum products (gone are oil changes, complicated transmissions, radiators and tune-ups). In four months we saved $855.00 in gasoline and paid $4.00 to the power company. Environmental responsibility has been profitable, saving a projected $5,500 per year in home and auto energy costs. Looking forward these costs are primary inflation factors eating into discretionary spending, especially for those on fixed incomes.

We explained to our caninus familiaris domesticus, Sammy, she has a cap on her allowable veterinary expenses so she has to take good care of herself. We told her $35: we might find the money if she really has a problem. She got the message and stayed healthy for more than 10 years.

While sharing coffee may seem cheap to some we prefer to think of ourselves as frugal. Dan's father was cheap with his coffee habit. He made one large pot of coffee lasting many days. He microwaved what he wanted and what was left he poured back. Seriously, his habits might have reflected his Scottish heritage of legendary thriftiness—he was the sole provider for six. Nobody went hungry and all were taken care of. He was an industrious example of developing his own mail-order businesses.

With the exception of our energy cost savings, perhaps some of this is overstated, but we reflect a big-picture attitude of conserving energy, food, water and encourage recycling. It's been reported Californians recycle up to half of their refuse, a good start. We grow some vegetables and buy the rest at the farmer's market, shop at thrift stores, and purchase for quality and take care of each item for years. Purchasing fresh vegetables locally is cheaper and healthier than canned, processed boxed foods and dairy products. Purchasing from many small businesses in the local community keeps the local economy thriving. When purchasing from a corporate retail chain store, your money ends up who knows where. If we didn't have this overall seamless philosophy, we might not have been so persistent in saving and building a nest egg.

Deductions and Vacations

We never saw most of our investment dollars—they came from regular payroll deductions deposited in our mutual funds. After the initial enrollment automatic payroll systems do the rest including tax reporting. This gift from the IRS and employers makes it easy to set aside money, more convenient than writing a check each month.

Whenever we received a raise we would add half of the increase to our deductions for retirement. We knew how powerful this decision could be. Likewise any tax refunds were split: half for retirement and half for vacations.

Over the years, we toured Russia, England, drove through Europe from Holland to Italy and New Zealand. We cruised the Mediterranean, Alaska, Hawaii and the Caribbean. Next is Vietnam where Steve earned his Purple Heart.

Take the opportunity to travel abroad. Don't wait until you retire. Around the world people want the same things we do: security, family, freedom, peace, health and prosperity. They work for their families, drive/bicycle/public transport/walk to their businesses or job and are eager to help with directions. English is spoken almost everywhere. You can find decent prices on cruises—a great way to relax and let somebody else take care of *all* the accommodations, serve exquisite cuisine, experience the calming sea, as you travel comfortably from one exotic location to another.

The positives outnumber the few negatives of traveling many times over. Most travelers would agree traveling increases well-being, opens the mind to new ideas and increases gratitude for our country. The rewards are more than a new car bought every three years could ever provide.

What Counts?

Not everything counts that can be counted,
not everything that can be counted, counts.

— Einstein

It's not about the most stuff, power or the most money. It's about working toward abundance in a way which provides rich experiences, connection with others and security. When we met we played racquetball, jogged and hiked. We completed three marathons, a couple of half marathons and many 10ks. Our major expenses were shoes and fried chicken after the race with friends. Those marathons kept us fit and reinforced the values of hard work, goal setting and early morning wake-up calls.

To get away we backpacked in the Sierras and climbed Mt. Whitney several times in our student years and later on. Dan retired in 2000 and *still* loves to hike, especially with Sammy. He climbed the organizational ladder and became the president of a popular L.G.B.T. hiking club, Great Outdoors—Los Angeles Chapter. With 300 members and friends we hiked the Angeles National Forest, coastal parks, desert, local mountains and the high Sierras north of Los Angeles in the middle of the state.

The connection to the wealth of experiences from nature through hiking and service is nothing new. Leadership and friendship through a shared love for the outdoors doesn't cost a lot. Hiking doesn't pollute the environment and has wholesome non-monetary rewards—the light breeze whistling through the pines, the coyote's "summons" to its peers, the cricket's chorus as night approaches and the cosmic hide and seek of the moon with the clouds. Nature's presence has been around for millions of years, long before humans and will remain long after.

Meanwhile, back in the city we understood the importance of containing housing and automobile expenses—two major purchases which cost hundreds of thousands of dollars during the working years. About 50 percent of family income goes to housing and transportation. Attention to these two major expenses account for the majority stake of achieving financial freedom.

Legendary billionaire investor Warren Buffett still lives in the same house he bought in 1958 for $31,500.

Housing

A popular question asked the Tooheys who authored the book *The Average Family's Guide to Financial Freedom* was how can a family of five survive in a one-bathroom house? Americans have collectively forgotten most people over 50 were raised in a one-bathroom house. Steve's family had an *outhouse* for a farm family of six (mom, dad, grandma and three children) until he was eight. What a luxury when his folks built *one indoor* bathroom in 1955. Dan was luckier, never used an outhouse. His family of six had the average number of indoor bathrooms at the time: one.

In the last generation, Americans spend more than they need for oversized housing with higher mortgage costs, higher taxes, higher maintenance and utilities— higher concomitant stress.

When we purchased our home on Mt. Washington in Los Angeles in 1981 we rented the downstairs spare bedroom and bath for several years in order to help pay the mortgage. Our 1,100 square-foot upstairs had two tiny baths, a small kitchen and no dining room. It was the perfect size for our budget.

Our bedroom consisted of a mattress on the floor with no drapes to shade the bright morning sun and used furniture throughout. Our house was quality built and withstood, unscathed, several earthquakes including the serious 1994 Northridge trembler. Designed and built by a student of Frank L. Wright in 1956, this streamlined moderne Prairie Style signature structure was in a decent neighborhood close to our jobs, with a top-rated public school, Mt. Washington Elementary, a block away. As with most purchases we bought quality and previously owned for the long-term. We lived in this home for 27 years.

Mortgage interest is a major expense with house purchases. Dan discovered $100 per month added to our 30-year home mortgage payment paid off the house in about 20 years. How fa-abulous. A new way to save—amazing—10 years off! The power of this small increase manifests when you compare the extra payment to the last 10 years of *no* payments. We were motivated to start paying down on our mortgage from day one and paid it off in 23 years. Not having a mortgage payment liberates us just as a dairy herd feels the first day of a Wisconsin spring, running around the pasture, gorging on virgin grass after being cooped up all winter. You'd feel better too after a winter diet of stale dry hay and corn silage. With that kind of freedom why pay the minimum?

When it came time to sell the value of our house quintupled, thanks to our local public school and the new Metro Gold line train station nearby. Nothing unique, Southern California real estate values increased several times in three decades.

What's the cost of a new car smell?

We couldn't afford the habit of buying a new car every three or four years. We knew cars cost a lot, but too many would argue "aren't appearances everything?" Perhaps for some, but those appearances are *not* long-term investments.

That egocentric argument is drenched in cultural bull. Daniel Quirk knows. He owned of one of the biggest car dealerships in New England. He said, "You know, it's one thing to save money but the purchase of a car is still an emotionally charged decision for most people…. Part of being an American is to have a little bit of gasoline in your veins."

> *That new car smell is the most*
> *expensive fragrance in the world.*
> **—Andrew Tobias, financial author.**

The new car culture remains strong. It doesn't matter one iota that new car values drop by 25 percent the minute we drive off the lot. This last century's love affair is uniquely American. A few trysts and one-night stands are no match for an American's personal identification with what's parked in the front driveway—the venerable and glittery muscle car—quintessence of status, power, and unwholesome independence. Unless gas prices reach $6 a gallon or more, as they do elsewhere on the planet, the "love affair" appears long lasting.

Ready for a little downshifting?

Financial planner and author Jonathan Pond conducted a study on car purchases in the 1990s. To nobody's surprise he found Americans are wasting money. He compiled statistics in conjunction with the American Automobile Association, using a 7.5 percent annual return on investment and a 3.5 percent inflation rate. Over a 40-year working career a hypothetical consumer who buys a new car and keeps it for 10 years will come out financially ahead of those folks who buy a new car every three years. By taking the savings in new car payments and insurance and investing it, allowing the money to compound over the decades, he reports the total would be about $385,000.

What a coincidence—our case-study methodology supports Pond's research. Keeping our cars for a long time helped us save about $300,000 in our 403(b)s. Why is our finding not a surprise when compared to Pond's results? Table 14 shows our combined 45-year driving life. Dan and I bought two new cars and the rest were used. Whether new, demo or used we kept each car for years.

Our car purchase history represents two guys who drove cars to get from here to there in Los Angeles, throughout California to Canada, Mexico and Wisconsin.

My car is so old that
when I fill it up with gas, its value doubles.
—Retired Nightly Business Report anchor Paul Kangas

Table 14

Steve's Car Purchases (All used, 1 demo)	Dan's Car Purchases (Lexus and Mitsubishi were new car purchases)
1966 Volkswagen paid $1,250	66 Volkswagen Hatchback paid $300
1982 Diesel VW (Demo) paid $7,000	1970 Volvo paid $3,500
1987 Jeep Wrangler paid $12,000	1978 Pontiac paid $7,500 (Demo)
1993 Lincoln Mark VIII paid $21,000	1986 Mitsubishi paid $16,000
1997 Sport Explorer paid $4,000 from a friend in 2005	1991 Explorer paid $18,000
	Still owns a 13 year-old 1999 Lexus 300SX, paid $38,000 (new).
Summary Steve paid about $45,250 and returned about $13,000 in trade-ins.	**Summary** Dan paid about $83,300 and returned about $6,000 in trade-ins.
We paid a total of approximately $128,550 on our combined car purchases and got back approximately $19,000 in trade-ins for a 45-year expenditure of $109,550.00.	

We omitted the cost of our recent Leaf purchase in 2012. The table illustrates purchases during our working years, when the negative effect of chronic new car purchases on retirement savings are indisputable.

Our total out-of-pocket car purchases of $109,550 over 45 years averaged $2,434 a year. We avoided most finance charges by paying cash.

> *Investing in our 403(b)s was instinctive:*
> *the thought of getting a set of new Beamers*
> *instead was preposterous.*
> **—The Authors**

Many think ongoing car payments are a fact of life. They aren't. The persistence of this habit is outrageously expensive as Pond reports. Wouldn't new car payments be better used for a child's college education, paying down the mortgage, credit cards or fund your retirement plan? Then the Joneses can feel permanently good with their bigger and newer gas-guzzler. You can terminate this unhealthy competition.

New vehicles are a primary source of people short-shrifting their retirement nest egg while adding to their debt. Find out for yourself. Keep your car for seven years after it's paid off. Let's exchange car payments for an IRA deposit and maybe take a trip to the country of your family's origin. At the risk of presenting a diatribe we want to stimulate discussion to support a family commitment to retirement savings.

Drinks are "On the House"

Steve drinks about a glass of wine or a mixed drink at home or with dinner about twice a month. Dan hasn't had a drink in 45 years. Let's examine an approximate cost of drinking two mixed drinks with each Saturday evening dinner for 37 years:

- Four mixed drinks each costing $3 per drink: $12 per Saturday dinner *(Note: averaged throughout three and one-half decades. Mixed drinks today cost about $6 to $7 and drinks 37 years ago cost about $1.50. We used a conservative, rough estimate of $3 per drink for illustration).*

- $48 per month (four Saturdays per month)

- $48.00 x 12 months = $576 per year.

- 37 years X $576 = $21,312 nominal savings.

If the $576 per year were invested with a conservative 5 percent interest rate, this money would grow to about $57,000. $576 invested in the S&P 500 index at 12% annually since 1975 grows to about $250,000. Consider two mixed drinks once a week is light social drinking. Imagine the cost of one drink per day.

What is so great about frugal living?

Plenty. Our families of origin provided money scrimping models and our social consciousness-raising experiences during the counterculture 1960s dovetailed seamlessly with a balanced, healthful and stress-free life. We spent less than what we earned and paid our debts quickly. We were able to continue our education in our thirties and forties, enhancing our careers with higher incomes.

Neither of us graduated with high honors in our academic careers from high school through college. We weren't valedictorians or voted "most likely to succeed." We don't sing show tunes or excel at design. We defined success with getting an education and everything else would fall into place. Education remained our best option. John Wooden (former UCLA coaching great) would agree when he wrote: "Our society tells us all that matters is, "Who's number one?" By this standard, most of us are losers…I think we all have the potential to be winners. We may or may not drive a bigger car, get a better grade, or score more points…But…the 'score' that matters most is the one that measures your effort…."

Dan's Special Education doctorate was funded by a state scholarship. He wrote job-training grants for people with disabilities and recovering alcoholics and administered those programs. Steve completed teacher training CSULA and also earned a doctorate from UCLA. Recall his mom saved Social Security for his first year of college. Then he paid his own way with help from the G. I. Bill and saving. We are grateful to the taxpayers for our excellent public education and Steve's mom for her financial and educational foresight.

Being frugal is the cornerstone of wealth-building.
—**Authors of *Millionaire Next Door***

The Millionaire Next Door

The journey of wealth accumulation by working class Americans has been documented in Thomas Stanley and William Danko's excellent insightful book, *The Millionaire Next Door*. They studied the living and working habits of regular people who started from *nothing* and became millionaires and multimillionaires. They chronicled how these people, many uneducated—who drive old cars, live in modest homes, wear clothes purchased at thrift stores—amassed sizable nest eggs.

Stanley and Danko found most American millionaires, for example, drive a Ford F-150 truck and "79 percent of the millionaires I have surveyed report when purchasing a home they sought a neighborhood that had excellent public schools." Warren Buffett proudly announced in a recent interview in *Time Magazine,* "No Buffett in Omaha has ever gone to a private school."

Stanley and Danko's book demonstrates that wealth is available to all, not just the image-conscious uber-rich who are chauffeured to the Hamptons. Their book uncovers the secrets of the lifestyle of the majority of American millionaires—that truck parked in the driveway, a neighborhood public school and dining at home in their finest—dungarees.

Common Sense is not so Common.

—Voltaire

These common sense savings recommendations are written in hundreds of financial books. Even the Bible documents money ideas in Proverbs: "Take care of the pence, and the pounds (scheckels) will take care of themselves." Before you roll your eyes, the common sense tips we quote throughout this book are valuable:

- Set a long-term retirement goal
- Learn how the financial system works
- Be patient and invest consistently, in good times and in bad
- Maintain a quality life: stay in touch with family, exercise, get plenty of quiet time and rest. Get outside (without a headset)

- Read

If you believe having a budget and balancing your checkbook works, do it. We didn't use a budget, it took too much time and was unnecessary. We paid ourselves first and spent the rest. That worked perfectly. The exact amount set aside remains a delicate balance only you can decide.

We are swollen with meaningless satisfactions and
dulled by petty immediacies.

–Norman Cousins

Resolutions

Saving can be a quiet responsible adult thing to do even if you're still wrestling with your impulsive and demanding inner child. We met this challenge with big picture values discussed in this chapter and by writing down New Year's resolutions. We report our list from 1988 as an example.

The goal categories are: Philosophical/spiritual, House, Recreation, Social, Professional, Financial and Physical. The tasks are many: dog training school, fix the doorbell, lose weight (ha-ha), pay down/off debt (be specific), attend live theatre, travel, gain computer skills, get the portfolio up to $(whatever) and many others. Write all the little things down. Written goals improve the chances of completion rather than leaving them to dance into the abyss of our minds. We wear these goals loosely—not a source of stress. Celebrate *all* achievements: difficult, easy and the inconsequential.

Simplicity, a thing most rare in our age.

—Ovid, Roman poet

In the big rush of work and family it's important to protect our inner space. Dan recalls a speaker many years ago who asked, "In the last quiet time of your life, what will you look back on?" Will it be a busy life taking care of a house too big, new cars with chronic payments and the latest boat, off-road vehicle, clothes or electronic gadgets?

You can be just as poor on 95 percent of your income,
so save 5 percent for the future.

—**The Authors**

Frugal Late-Bloomers?

This chapter shows how the good idea of saving can be accomplished. Nobody has to earn MBAs, financial advisor certification, or pursue ordination as a priest, Rabbi, mullah or a minister to achieve financial freedom. If a third of your retirement pot comes from contributions, another third from car and house cost savings and the last third from low cost investing, you should be on track.

It's not a stretch to recall intuitively that most of us Boomer and older generations were raised in modest circumstances in a one bathroom house. Even though the word frugal wasn't spoken, our frugal minded parents were no different than most parents who try to live simply. Most of us grew up knowing "save-for-a-rainy-day" and "don't-spend-more-than-you-earn" remain great ideas. But as adults many of us succumb to the popular cultural pressure of consumerism— bigger and better. You have probably figured out when it comes to frugal living or idealism, we weren't late-bloomers. Did you get the frugal bug early on too?

CHAPTER 14

Why Plan for Retirement?

Not all of us would quit our job today, even if we could. But that choice has a nice ring to it. It might provide an alternative in a world when life comes *at us* unannounced and uninvited: to care for a loved one, recover after a natural disaster or maybe to get out of an intolerable employment (or personal) situation. Serious illness and injury also have a way of refocusing life's choices, although we prefer not to think about these unpleasant realities.

If you had a choice to stop working four to five years sooner than you anticipated with enough money to supplement your Social Security or pension, would you do it? Heck, who wouldn't? What's more exciting than the full-time pursuit of activities you value with passion, supported by financial freedom?

Chance or Choice?

If your ship doesn't come in, swim out to it.
—Jonathan Winters

Financial freedom left to chance is risky. Our fortunes are not so much a matter of chance. Luck stays in Las Vegas—we know *that* consequence. Fortunes come from informed choices: not to be anticipated but to be sought after by planning for the long term. What inspiration does it take to get started? Two words might inspire even the most cynical workaholic among us.

I Quit!

While Steve loved his 24-year career as a public elementary teacher and technology adviser, he quit. We hear about people afraid of losing their jobs; but we rarely hear about the empowerment of people who say, "enough is enough," especially as they near retirement. Most of us don't think we can quit our jobs. If we commit to a positive goal, it can be done. So it's not just about having the personal power to quit—it's more.

Retirement is a Positive Thing

Retirement living *is* wonderful. We looked forward to it for years. The mental picture alone provided plenty of motivation to plan. Our steady thinking about retirement kept us focused.

If you believe retirement is dreadful, then it's unlikely you'll plan for it. Ask family members or friends who retired if they like it. Like it? Chances are they love it. This chapter provides some of the reasons why we planned for life after work.

Yes, there's a full life after the career. Steve credits his baby-boomer generation for revolutionizing retirement from sitting in a rocking chair to active lifestyles. We continue many of the affirming hobbies discussed in the last chapter started while we were working. Now we do them full-time including our newest full-time hobby, writing this book.

Location, Location, Location

Since buying our desert vacation condo thirty years ago we planned on living in the desert southwest. We love the serenity and the visuals: Irish green golf courses, rich desert flora and the boulevards lined by countless elegant palm trees. Visitors often comment on the easy pace, beauty and peace here as they soak up each minute of relief from their back home work and routines: snow removal or combating dreary rain.

Don't you love the positive images of a valley, any valley? Coachella is no exception. Bordered by two 11,000 foot mountains, Mt. San Jacinto and San Gorgonio, the water run-off provides year round produce and an aquifer augmenting our water needs. Yes, July and August bring out the minimalist in us permanent residents, but the serenity is deepened as the temperatures rise with the deep blue sky. There are always those nearby mountains for a break from the mesmerizing stillness of 100-plus temperatures.

Social Safety Nets?

If you're younger than fifty you are concerned social security might not survive when your day comes. Private and public pension plans are being squeezed by tight money throughout the nation. Unbalanced retirement plans (100 percent stocks) lost 40 percent and more in 2008, thanks to Wall Street and unbalanced 401(k) portfolios.

Buying into the lazy portfolio strategy at a young age provides an advantage because of added years to grow the portfolio. Younger workers will need it—demographic experts predict more of us will live to 100 years in the next decade or two, a scary impetus.

Educators must work 38 or more years to qualify for 100 percent salary from pension benefits. The media pundits give the impression all teachers (and public workers) receive 100 percent salary benefit from pension plans, "great giveaways." *Wrong*—Steve receives 49 percent of his teacher's salary. His benefit is below the average because he only worked for 24 years and retired at 60 (btw, he's *not* complaining). According to CalSTRS the average benefit for California teachers is about 60 percent of salary or about $48,000 per year before taxes.

Steve's first principal worked for 58 years and retired at age 83. He cherished his career, lucky he stayed healthy and motivated. So he didn't need to plan. His risk paid off. Any California public school educator with that many years of service credit will earn 100% salary.

According to many news reports, 64 percent of all retirees live only on their Social Security benefit. In 2010, the average Social Security benefit was about $14,000 per year.

—The Week

Not everyone can or wants to work that long. Our friend Chris is talented, dedicated and a fine primary teacher. He's bilingual, earned the prestigious National Board Certificate (NBC) and earns a good salary. He has been a teacher since day one and is at the top of the pay scale.

Unlike Steve's former principal who remained excited and motivated Chris is exhausted at age 46. He regrets he has lost his enthusiasm. If he accepts an out of the classroom position to recharge his batteries he'll lose the NBC deferential, a steep salary decrease. The earliest he can retire with pension benefits is nine years, and he won't receive 100 percent salary even after teaching for 30 years.

Risky Business

Private pensions are at risk. Private company defined benefit plans decreased from serving 30 percent of the national workforce down to fewer than 18 percent. The future of these retirement benefits remains uncertain. Even if pension plans (and Social Security) were financially solid for the foreseeable future, neither is designed to provide 100% financial security for all employees, public or private.

Consider these six specific risks:

- According to the Employee Benefits Research Institute, "Forty seven percent of all employees retired sooner than originally planned."

- When a retirement date is determined by a *formula and years of service* your choices vanish. You give up optimal options at your psychological, mental or physical peril.

- By not using your employer sponsored tax-deferred plan, you may pay more income taxes than those who use the plan.

- Relying on a pension as the sole source of income requires working for the same employer for many years. Both pension and social security need to be supplemented. Most of us cannot or will not work into our 70s and beyond.

- Few of us can work when burned-out. An otherwise successful and fulfilling career can change to a discouraging and unrewarding drudgery.

- Expecting an inheritance appears to be a sensible substitute for not having a money management plan. However, expecting parents to fund adult children's retirement is dangerously myopic. Inheritance is hardly bereft of emotion, sibling enmity and disappointment.

What Can a Late-Bloomer Do?

Plenty. You have been reading this book—we show in great detail how it's possible to start late and succeed. Ok, some admit you haven't saved a dime and not lived below your means, but many 50-year-olds still have the possibility of saving $325,000 or more.

Late as it is you can start setting aside money with

retirement looming and some bones begin to creak. This may compel a constructive start. Fund your plan now. Keep funding it.

If you are over 50 the "catch-up" features of your employer's retirement plan are terrific. If you qualify for the catch-up, max them out. For example, if you invest the 2013 max with $17,500 per year contributions and make a conservative three percent annual yield in the investment, when 65 rolls around you will have $325,667. So take heart, it can be done.

If $17,000 per year starting is out of reach, pick a reasonable amount to save, say eight percent of your salary. Table 15 illustrates smaller annual contributions: $5,000 and $10,000.

Table 15		
Annual contributions for 15 years. Starting at age 50 and ending with a probable total saved at age 65		
Annual Contributions to a tax-deferred plan	**Average Annual Performance***	**Probable Total saved at age 65**
$5,000	3.0 percent	$95,784
$10,000	3.0 percent	$191,569
$17,500 (*Max in 2013*)	3.0 percent	$335,245
*Before costs, assuming a low-cost plan.		

Notice the $5,000 for 15 years amounts to over $95,000. Most Americans have much less than $95,000 saved. Never feel $95,000 is miniscule.

How does this "late-start" plan supplement your social security or pension? Let's calculate what the total amounts might do for you. Table 16 illustrates the distribution phase starting at age 65 when you retire.

Table 16			
Hypothetical annual monthly incomes in distribution phase of the different supplemental nest eggs.			
Nest egg amount from Table 15	**Interest Yield During Retirement**	**Annual Income in Retirement**	**Monthly Income in Retirement**
$95,784	3.0 %	$2,873.52	**$239.46***
$191,569	3.0 %	$5,747.07	**$478.92***
$335,245	3.0%	$10,057.35	**$838.11***
*Ordinary income taxes must be paid and costs are not subtracted. Figures are illustrations only.			

Depending on how much you contribute, that $239.46, $478.92 or $814.17 supplements your pension or social security. It doesn't look bad, considering you haven't touched the principle. This interest bearing income continues for the rest of your life.

We calculate a conservative annual return of 3%

for illustrative purposes. Your account, the return and the monthly supplemental income might be higher if you invest using one of the lazy portfolios. Finding lazy portfolio type funds from your employer's selection may be difficult. However, by using the Roth IRA, you are free to set up a lazy portfolio plan on your own and there are no taxes due when you take it out in retirement. People over 50 can invest up to $6000 a year. You will have to pay ordinary income taxes for funds going into the Roth IRA.

Some people go through a physical exam every year, yet ignore the recommendations which will alleviate their ills. Intuitively we know this is unwise but each of us has experienced this intransigence. Starting from scratch to save for retirement is a major commitment, made easier with a supportive partner.

If common sense, wise counsel, protection of loved ones, and the natural law of self-preservation aren't enough to rein in excessive spending, induce people to save, and work out a sensible plan, what is?
—Lee Eisenberg, *The Number*

Start with specific goals, live below your means and increase contributions over time. The act of saving and investing brings its own sense of comfort and security by reducing the consequences of spending at (or beyond) your means. Insurance, social security or a pension alone can't duplicate the peace of mind provided by your proactive management of finances.

Advanced planning can mollify life's unplanned challenges. Retirement planning allows for emergencies, discretionary savings and having money for those surprise expenses, worry free. Knowing you have saved a nest egg in addition to your employer's pension plan and social security provides a sense of security and freedom. If inheritance is a reality, those extra funds will fit into the existing plan with additional financial freedom—less temptation to spend it needlessly. When you decide, you can do the unthinkable and quit.

The decision to start and take control of our own retirement plan was *never* a mistake. It's one of the best decisions we made and you won't regret it either.

*In every crises
lies the seed
of opportunity*

Denouement

We've shared our financial "late-bloomer" story. As two frugal guys from modest beginnings we became a couple in 1975. Our hippie values cemented our relationship, bolstered by mentors. Even then we had our eyes set on the long-term. Education and saving were paramount--we knew we had to take care of our future.

After a phase with annuity products we discerned the sham and graduated to mutual funds. The sweeping energy of the technology revolution and bubble captured us—we enjoyed the rise of tech stocks and funds, excited by the tremendous growth and sickened by our immense loss. Between 1995 and October, 2002 we made and lost a million. Yes, we were late bloomers in our late 50s, in an urgent fix. With the application of what we learned from many financial authors we were able to gain back our lost money. What we lost in the tech bubble we regained during the real estate bubble through asset class diversification, low cost active and passive strategies and bonds.

Most crises have a seed of opportunity. The bursting of the tech bubble enervated us to discover reasonable options for retirement savings. With respect for stock market uncertainty came increasing patience and the revelation of the inexorable strength of investing in worldwide economies.

This is a synopsis of what we found:

- Pay yourself first
- Discern objective information from sales pitches
- Long-term thinking pertaining to risk has to be lived, not taught
- Take advantage of tax deferment opportunities
- Petition your employer for low-cost funds that fit their available plan (403(b), 401(k), 457(b))
- Live below one's means, knowing why helps us stay motivated
- Require transparency: know the costs of buying and selling before signing -- don't sign what you don't understand
- Invest in broad asset classes: overall market averages beat managed funds over 70% of the time according to research.
- 70% of participants erroneously believe their employer's retirement plan is free.
- Use websites to independently verify fund costs
- Use the lazy portfolios to assist allocation decisions
- Investing errors center around the lack of diversification and excessive risk. Common spending errors are expensive housing and frequent car purchases.
- Match the percentage of your bond allocation to your age
- Bypass Wall Street firms, their fiduciary interest is to themselves, not you
- Don't jockey for the next trendy stock, buy them all
- Learn to locate and work with a fiduciary advisor who signs the fiduciary oath: pay the hourly fee
- Be prepared before meeting with your fiduciary adviser

- Couples: share this process as you understand it--express differences, unearth mistakes without blaming, compromise/truce, celebrate proactive moves and take advantage of a fiduciary adviser
- The bulk of market gains comes from astute control of costs: compounded costs can devour about a third of your final nest egg (see Appendix D)
- Diversify: asset classes rise and fall, therefore diversify across many classes to minimize the effects of bubbles, crashes and everyday fluctuations
- An ethical "sale" or "deal" benefits *both* parties

A proactive mindset is essential: investing in yourself by learning the basics you can discern legitimate advice, investigate funds (use the ticker symbol), recognize your employer's options and rest easier. Much of our nestegg was made possible by controlling three costs: autos, housing and investment expenses. Trust that the worldwide economies grow over the long term.

These ideas come together as a mosaic to alleviate fears when the market frets. Tough times will challenge the need to hold to a plan, but these times pass. The emotional ringer can be relentless without a plan, making some investors jump around desperately trying to be *right* when it's better to be *still*. This effort can foster peace of mind during inconsistent markets.

The investment process is an obtuse, complicated, and frustrating adventure -- it can be revolutionary too. You are on your way to untangling the morass, congratulations! We found comfort and abundance in these discoveries. We are grateful for our journey and believe it can help newbies and late-bloomers.

—Best of Fortunes

Acknowledgements

We had a lot of help. The impetus for writing this book came partly from frustration with the sales people who misled us followed by those who inspired us toward a solution. We made friends along the way who shared their investing stories and added to our early learning adventure: Sandy Keaton, Joe MacDonald, Chris Evans, Dean Cohen, Crystal Mendez, Brad Rumble, and all LAUSD educators.

John Bogle's crusade has attracted a legion of indexing advocates whose contributions to Boogleheads.org and whose books gave direction and organization to this effort: Taylor Larimore, Mel Lindauer, Adrian Nenu and numerous other financially savvy Bogleheads and authors who helped us change direction in our late 50s.

We are particularly indebted to Scotty Dauenhauer,

our fiduciary advisor who followed-up with specific direction for our investment choices at a critical time in our learning curve while helping on an early draft and some of the calculations in this manuscript. Additional thanks to Robert Machado, Compass Rose Financial Planning, for verifying our calculations.

We thank financial columnists Kathy Kristof and Paul Lim for listening and writing about Steve's challenges with his employer's investment offerings. Debora Vrana of the Los Angeles Times Makeover Feature gave us a boost by accepting us to be featured in her article. We thank author Dr. William Bernstein and friends Karen Reyes and Phil Mortimer for their comments, encouragement and guidance.

The Palm Springs Guild critique group made a valiant effort to improve our writing skills, but any blunders are strictly our own. We are grateful to Jim Duggin, Steve Scott, Irene Tritel, Fritzie Von Jessen, Fran and Harold Kaplan and Linda Smith for their forbearance and frequent patience. We thank our editors, John Carrigan, Bonnie Smith and Jeff Wuorio, for their top notch professional expertise. We are especially indebted to Jeff for changing the direction of an early manuscript that was going nowhere fast.

Mark Edward Anderson, AquaZebra, designed the beautiful cover and interior layout reflecting our message tastefully while advising us of the many steps involved in moving our book into publication. Kudos to Larry Merkle for his photographic acumen that brought out our best.

Our parents provided the best values of all: sense of humor, appreciation of nature, balance, living below our means and consistent saving. We didn't forget a vital lesson—the one-bathroom house was sufficient. As young adults we listened to our mentors Sy Krinski, Dave Bilovsky, Burt Alperson and John Boldt who taught us to untangle and accept life's riddles as responsible adults.

Not least of all we celebrate our collaboration— rehashing our differences, reliving our financial memories, and putting this all together, sometimes with hyperbole: often under the kind umbrellas of Peet's and Starbucks Coffee Houses. And finally, thank you Sammy, our loyal hairy friend for keeping us company all along.

Appendices

Appendix A

Vanguard portfolio allocation models
Income

100% bonds

0% Stocks

100% Bonds

0% Short-term reserves

Historical risk/return (1926–2011)

Average annual return	5.6%
Best year (1982)	32.6%
Worst year (1969)	–8.1%
Years with a loss	13 of 86

20% stocks/80% bonds

20% Stocks

80% Bonds

0% Short-term reserves

Historical risk/return (1926–2011)

Average annual return	6.7%
Best year (1982)	29.8%
Worst year (1931)	–10.1%
Years with a loss	12 of 86

30% stocks/70% bonds

30% Stocks

70% Bonds

0% Short-term reserves

Historical risk/return (1926–2011)

Average annual return	7.3%
Best year (1982)	28.4%
Worst year (1931)	–14.2%
Years with a loss	14 of 86

Vanguard portfolio allocation models
Balanced

40% stocks/60% bonds

40% Stocks

60% Bonds

0% Short-term reserves

Historical risk/return (1926–2011)

Average annual return	7.8%
Best year (1933)	27.9%
Worst year (1931)	−18.4%
Years with a loss	16 of 86

50% stocks/50% bonds

50% Stocks

50% Bonds

0% Short-term reserves

Historical risk/return (1926–2011)

Average annual return	8.2%
Best year (1933)	32.3%
Worst year (1931)	−22.5%
Years with a loss	17 of 86

60% stocks/40% bonds

60% Stocks

40% Bonds

0% Short-term reserves

Historical risk/return (1926–2011)

Average annual return	8.6%
Best year (1933)	36.7%
Worst year (1931)	−26.6%
Years with a loss	21 of 86

Vanguard portfolio allocation models

Growth

70% stocks/30% bonds

70% Stocks	
30% Bonds	
0% Short-term reserves	

Historical risk/return (1926–2011)	
Average annual return	9.0%
Best year (1933)	41.1%
Worst year (1931)	–30.7%
Years with a loss	22 of 86

80% stocks/20% bonds

80% Stocks	
20% Bonds	
0% Short-term reserves	

Historical risk/return (1926–2011)	
Average annual return	9.4%
Best year (1933)	45.4%
Worst year (1931)	–34.9%
Years with a loss	23 of 86

100% stocks

100% Stocks	
0% Bonds	
0% Short-term reserves	

Historical risk/return (1926–2011)	
Average annual return	9.9%
Best year (1933)	54.2%
Worst year (1931)	–43.1%
Years with a loss	25 of 86

Appendix A used with the permission of the Vanguard Group.

Appendix B

A Detailed Look at our Core Holdings

This asset allocation is the expanded version of Figure 18 at the end of Chapter Eight (page 134). This portfolio served us as expected for the past four years-- allowing for growth with some exposure to risk. It took several years to set this up.

Our five core holdings should be familiar to you:

- The **first** core holding is the total stock market fund **(VTSMX)** which primarily invests in large cap companies.

- We augment this with the **second** core holding, the **extended market index (VEXMX)** which includes both mid-cap and small-cap to broaden our total domestic stock holdings.

- The **third** core holding is the total international stock market fund **(VGTSX)** which is supplemented by emerging markets **(VEIEX or VE-MAX)**, invested in recently developed industrial countries. With these funds, we are exposed to equities worldwide.

- Our **fourth** core holding is the total bond market index **(VBTLX)**, invested in corporate, long-term bonds and GNMAs. We include additional bond funds to broaden diversification within the bond allocation: Treasury Inflation Protection bonds, or TIPS **(VAIPX)**, GNMAs **(VFIIX, VFIJX)**, intermediate treasuries **(VFIUX)** and intermediate investment grade bonds **(VFICX, VFIDX)** which have lower interest rate risk than long-term bonds. Most are rated AA or greater. We don't have municipal or global bonds. We indicate two tickers where a lower expense kicks in for investing more money in a fund. As a portfolio grows Vanguard lowers the expense to their customers.

- Dan likes Loomis Sayles Bond (LSBRX - retail fee; LSBDX - institutional fee). It provides consistent competitive monthly returns. We prefer corporate bonds for the extra risk and return. For example, Loomis Sayles Bond dropped 21.8 percent in 2008, its second and worst decline in 20 years, scaring some investors into panic selling. That is a huge decline for a bond fund, but still not as volatile as equities. Corporate bonds pay higher rates for a reason: they are more risky than government bonds. Fortunately for those investors who didn't lose their long-term thinking, Loomis recovered with an astonishing 37.2 percent in 2009 and continues to grow. Dan never sold. By the way, during Loomis's decline in NAV Dan's monthly distribution remained steady. Why? Bonds keep paying regardless of the NAV. The payout changes little.

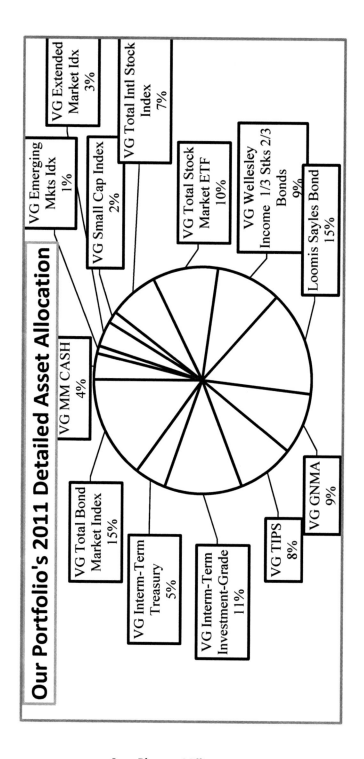

Our Portfolio's 2011 Detailed Asset Allocation

- VG Extended Market Idx 3%
- VG Total Intl Stock Index 7%
- VG Emerging Mkts Idx 1%
- VG Small Cap Index 2%
- VG Total Stock Market ETF 10%
- VG Wellesley Income 1/3 Stks 2/3 Bonds 9%
- Loomis Sayles Bond 15%
- VG MM CASH 4%
- VG Total Bond Market Index 15%
- VG Interm-Term Treasury 5%
- VG Interm-Term Investment-Grade 11%
- VG TIPS 8%
- VG GNMA 9%

Vanguard Wellesley (**VWIAX**) is our **fifth** and newest core holding. Over the next five to seven years as we both enter our 70s we will gradually transfer assets into Wellesley. This fund is excellent for retirees because it invests in dividend stocks and highly rated bonds. It is an income generating fund.

All funds are in Vanguard, Loomis Sayles and TIAA CREF. Steve likes TIAA-CREF cash holding because it was a 403(b) choice offered by his employer. TIAA-CREF and Vanguard provide interactive websites which give practical advice, offer online allocation changes, and have brokerage windows and accessible human support for forms and proper transfer procedures.

Appendix C

Short-term Thinking: Sales Pitches	Long-term Thinking: Objective Information
1. Frequent buying or selling securities.	1. Creating a plan and sticking with it.
2. Sold an annuity. Investor is not owning anything.	2. Purchasing an investment. The investor is part owner of the entire economy.
3. Active Strategy (aka active management strategy).	3. Passive Strategy (aka index investing).
4. Actively Managed Funds.	4. Index funds (aka passive investing).
5. Adviser/Investment Guru/Famous Manager's responsibility.	5. Individual responsibility with assistance of a fee only fiduciary financial adviser.
6. Complicated, exclusive, unique and "sophisticated" Plan.	6. Simple Plan, easily explained and understood by client.
7. One way communication from adviser to client.	7. Two-way communication with adviser with fiduciary responsibilities. Client is responsible for their plan.

8. The Market is Inefficient. Sales pitches are focused on exploiting market anomalies to get rich quickly.	8. Efficient Market Hypothesis/Modern Portfolio Theory. Slowly growing wealth over time
9. Information from insurance agent/broker/adviser.	9. Information/discussion from Internet, books and/or from a fee-only fiduciary adviser
10. Invest in only US Domestic equities, REITS or bonds. Focus on "hot" stock or fund.	10. Global Investing in equities, REITS, and bonds.
11. Sectors with great past and/or present performance.	11. Broad diversification across asset classes (Small, Mid, Large Cap; REITS, Bonds, International)
12. Predicting/Timing the market. Focus on prices and immediate past performance.	12. Sticking with Plan. Focus on strategy of reducing risk.
13. Overly Aggressive exciting portfolio (Bull market only).	13. Diversified boring portfolio.
14. Owning Individual Company Stocks.	14. Owning diversified portfolio of stock funds and bonds with rebalancing when needed.
15. Investing experience is fun, active, dynamic (Bull Market), "I am confident in my abilities!"	15. Investing is routine and balanced with your overall life activities.
16. Investing experience is consuming and terrible (Bear market), "I was ripped off by the system!"	16. Investing is routine and balanced with your overall life activities.

17. Vulnerable by excessive fees, risky investments and "too good to be true" performance.	17. Protected by self education.
18. Rarely/never looking at Portfolio or Tracking portfolio every single day.	18. Rebalancing When Needed.
19. Afraid of foreign investments and invest only in U.S. Domestic Equities.	19. Includes international equities, bonds, REITS, ETFs.
20. Picking investments primarily based on the hype of past performance and future prediction.	20. Past performance and future predictions are unimportant and categorically ignored.
21. Strive for a perfect portfolio that beats the benchmarks.	21. Strive for a diversified portfolio in which risk reflects the investors situation (age and tolerance).
22. Employee bargaining units either endorsing specific expensive vendors and financial planners or ignore that an employer sponsored plan exists.	22. Bargaining units can find consultants with fiduciary responsibility to offer objective information and transparency of fees by following ERISA 404c guidelines.
23. Investing in individual stocks, sectors and managed funds.	23. Investing in broad economies.
24. Self-interested professionally led and biased--conflict of interests abounds.	24. Non professional, self help led and objective--NO CONFLICT OF INTEREST, None!

#		
25.	Begins a conversation with a fiduciary financial adviser with a passive strategy philosophy.	Investor trusting the financial adviser, broker or insurance agent.
26.	Information addressing each investors risk tolerance, a plan and financial goals.	Misled by sales pitches claiming one thing or another.
27.	Investors are treated by Vanguard as "clients."	Investors are treated by brokers as customers or "Muppets."
28.	Think Long Term buy and hold with rebalancing.	Think short term trading and speculation.
29.	Wall Street noise is a cheap form of entertainment to get people to TRADE and trade often.	Relies on Wall Street Mania, business news, the "monkey mind" NOISE.
30.	Opting for benchmark returns with an intrinsically unexciting portfolio.	Hoping to beat the benchmarks/constantly searching for THE gimmick.
31.	Transparency of information including all costs.	Omission of important (total fees) information.
32.	Financial future will always be uncertain, risky, surprising, humbling (at times) and capricious.	Believe that the financial future is predictable and certain.
33.	Can honestly and courageously assess when we don't know.	Have a terrible time admitting we don't know.

34. Deal with mistakes and move on.	Can not admit that you are your worst enemy.
35. Building Wealth over a lifetime of working and saving with a plan.	Getting Rich quickly.
36. Living a meaningful and full life *within your means*.	Save every penny (miser) or borrow and spend, living from paycheck to paycheck.
37. Investment fees (along with risk assessment) are the number 1 priority in setting up your plan.	Investing fees are immaterial.
38. Like the financial media, ignore consumerism.	Embracing, believing, living and spending with the consumer culture.
39. Expense ratios are the best predictors of performance.	12b(1) fees are for marketing and management.
40. Investments and speculations are never the same!	Investments and speculations are the same thing.
41. Buy and hold. Rebalance when needed.	Trade and chase performance frequently.
42. Keep investments and insurance needs separate.	Mixing Investments with Insurance.

43. Financial market future performance is unknown and random.	Financial market future performance have *predictable* patterns.
44. Market is efficient. The anomalies cannot be predicted and are quickly corrected.	Market is inefficient and the anomalies are easily exploited for your benefit.
45. Fiduciary fee-only professional must put the interests of clients first.	Professional management's number 1 priority is to sell and get a stream of fees from you.
46. Hire a Fee only adviser and pay by the hour like all other professional services.	Hire a commission based adviser, broker from a brokerage firm or an insurance agent.
47. TIAA-CREF and Vanguard serve their clients needs at cost. They have one master: The clients.	Mutual fund companies are owned by management and shareholders.
48. Reducing risk and costs are the priority.	Performance to beat the market averages is the priority.
49. No mathematical analysis known today can predict future returns accurately and consistently.	Endless Portfolio quantitative analyses: Beta, Alpha, R-Squared, Monte Carlo, Sharp Ratio.
50. Learn from *your* mistakes, adjust portfolio accordingly and move on.	Denying, avoiding and blaming others for your portfolio decline.
51. Know the crucial difference between sales pitches vs. objective financial information.	Sales pitches from dark suited, good looking professionals are gospel truisms.

52. Using reams of past performance calculations, fund managers bios and star ratings to decide.	52. Never use past performance, star ratings and fund mangers information to decide on a fund.
53. Source of Financial Information is bias towards the professional's self interests.	53. Source of Financial Information is objective for the individual investor's self interest.
54. Never settle for market AVERAGES: Averages are too low.	54. The long term goal is average market returns.
55. Financial advisers are committed to portfolio charges and commissions on trades.	55. Ethical Financial Advisers accept fiduciary responsibility and are committed to your best interest.
56. Reluctant to challenge the authority of the financial professional.	56. Always Ask Questions about fees, services, philosophy, indexing vs. managing.
57. The Financial Management Profession is the most lucrative profession in the world (KPMG consultant).	57. The Financial Management Profession is STILL the most lucrative profession in the world.
58. Picking a financial adviser based on their credentials, experiences and past portfolio performance.	58. Selecting a financial adviser with credentials and experience who signs a fiduciary oath.
59. 100% non-ownership products such as insurance products or 100% bond portfolio.	59. Ownership products--indexed low cost equity index in combination with bond index funds.
60. "We will never accept any loss in your money."	60. Temporary loses in your portfolio give you the opportunity to make full market returns.

61. Buying a overly safe or overly risky security.	61. Holding a portfolio of securities where the risk exposure of bonds equals your age.
62. "Interest rates are going up. Better get an annuity."	62. Purchase short or intermediate maturity bonds.
63. "Your pension plan is in financial trouble, invest with me."	63. "Who told you that? Report this adviser to his or her company and your pension plan board.
64. "We are always transparent!"	64. "Here is a chart which shows the long term effect of fees on your final nest egg."
65. "We are fiduciaries!"	65. "This is a fiduciary oath signed by me. Let me explain what this means."

Appendix D

After years of studying costs we are always stunned by the enormity of how a couple of percentage points devastates a final nest egg. How much does a 2.25 percent fee **compounded** cost over 25 years?

Part A illustrates the difference between a 2.25 percent versus a 0.25 percent charge. Our hypothetical portfolio is the result of $10,000 invested every year for 25 years, earning an average annual return of 6 percent. I don't know about you but that difference ($142,358) is amazing. If we want the $560,171 nest egg we must watch costs.

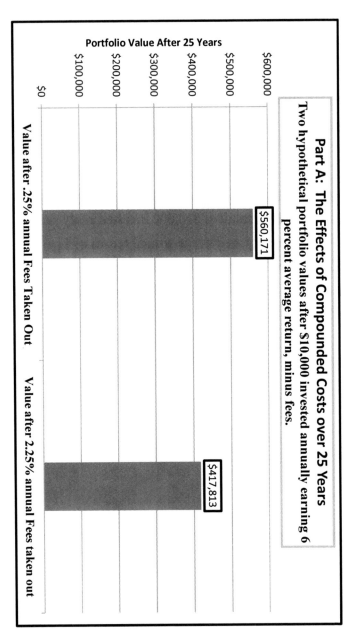

Part A: The Effects of Compounded Costs over 25 Years

Two hypothetical portfolio values after $10,000 invested annually earning 6 percent average return, minus fees.

Portfolio Value After 25 Years

$560,171

$417,813

Value after .25% annual Fees Taken Out

Value after 2.25% annual Fees taken out

Part B illustrates the progression of high and low fees over 25 years in five-year increments using the same data as in Part A.

Appendix D

| | **Part B: Compounded Costs over 25 Years** | | | |
| | **How 1/3 of Final Nest Egg is Lost to Fees!** | | | |
Year	Value of Portfolio after 2.25% Fees	Value of Portfolio after 0.25% Fees	Difference in Costs	Difference of high fees and low fees in Percent Lost.
1	$10,375	$10,575	$200	1.93%
5	$55,914	$59,315	$3,401	6.08%
10	$123,129	$137,761	$14,632	11.88%
15	$203,927	$241,507	$37,580	18.43%
20	$301,055	$378,713	$77,658	25.80%
25	$417,813	$560,171	**$142,358**	**34.07%**

We calculated what the investor pays per month at 2.25% over 25 years for a total cost of $142,358. We then divided the total cost by 25 years to get the annual cost ($5,695) divided again by 12 for a monthly average cost of $474. Notice in year one the cost difference between the rates is only $200. As the years go by the fees compound *substantially.* After 25 years this hypothetical investor paid over a third of their portfolio, 34.07 percent, stolen by the excess 2.25 percent fee.

The 1/3 reduction of the final nest egg finding has been replicated in many studies. A recent study by a public policy research group, Demos, found a median-income, two-earner family will lose, on average, roughly $155,000 to mutual fund costs through their 401(k) investments over the course of their careers. Bogle calls this "the tyranny of compound costs" and makes this point repeatedly in his books.

If required to write a monthly check for $474.00 we doubt any sane person would agree to such a ludicrous contract. But in the financial world this is *common practice*—starting at $200 and increasing over 25 years is ever so easily and automatically subtracted out of *our assets* without notice or fanfare. How nice they make it, so expedient and *quiet*. Long-term costs are rarely presented in the vast majority of financial planning workshops. One wonders why....

Part C: What are your Assets Under Management (AUM) costs in dollars?
It's important to know what you are paying over time.

Your Portfolio $?	$?	$?	$?	$?
Multiply by:	3.00%	1.95%	1.35%	0.35% Or Your Cost
2008				
2009				
2010				
2011				
2012				
Total Costs				

Appendix E*

Fiduciary Oath
National Association of Personal Financial Advisors

The advisor shall exercise his/her best efforts to act in good faith and in the best interests of the client.

The advisor shall provide written disclosure to the client prior to the engagement of the advisor, and thereafter throughout the term of the engagement, of any conflicts of interest, which will or reasonably may compromise the impartiality or independence of the advisor.

The advisor, or any party in which the advisor has a financial interest, does not receive any compensation or other remuneration that is contingent on any client's purchase or sale of a financial product.

The advisor does not receive a fee or other compensation from another party based on the referral of a client or the client's business.

Following the NAPFA Fiduciary Oath means I shall:

- Always act in good faith and with candor.
- Be proactive in disclosing any conflicts of interest that may impact a client.
- Not accept any referral fees or compensation contingent upon the purchase or sale of a financial product.

Signed this _____ of _____

_____
NAPFA-Registered Financial Advisor

CODE OF ETHICS

Objectivity: NAPFA members strive to be as unbiased as possible in providing advice to clients, and NAPFA members practice on a Fee-Only basis.

Confidentiality: NAPFA members shall keep all client data private, unless authorization is received from the client to share it. NAPFA members shall treat all documents with care and take care when disposing of them. Relations with clients shall be kept private.

Competence: NAPFA members shall strive to maintain a high level of knowledge and ability. Members shall attain continuing education at least at the minimum level required by NAPFA. Members shall not provide advice in areas where they are not capable.

Fairness & Suitability: Dealings and recommendation with clients will always be in the client's best interests. NAPFA members put their clients first.

Integrity & Honesty: NAPFA members will endeavor to always take the high road and to be ever mindful of the potential for misunderstanding that can accrue in normal human interactions. NAPFA members will be diligent to keep actions and reactions so far aboveboard that a thinking client or other professional would not doubt intentions. In all actions, NAPFA members should be mindful that in addition to serving our clients, we are about the business of building a profession, and our actions should reflect this.

Regulatory Compliance: NAPFA members will strive to maintain conformity with legal regulations.

Full Disclosure: NAPFA members shall fully describe method of compensation and potential conflicts of interest to clients and also specify the total cost of investments.

Professionalism: NAPFA members shall conduct themselves in a way that would be a credit to NAPFA at all times. NAPFA membership involves integrity, honest treatment of clients, and treating people with respect.

MISSION

To promote the public interest by advancing the financial planning profession and supporting our members consistent with our core values.

*Used with permission from the National Association of Personal Financial Advisors.

Glossary

12b (1) fee—A mutual fund expense in which the fund charges a portion of your assets to pay for marketing costs. This fee is included in the expense table of the fund's prospectus. Avoid funds that charge this fee.

401(k), 403(b), 457(b) plan—company-sponsored retirement plans in which employees make tax-deferred contributions from their salary, sometimes matched by the employer. Public sector 403(b) and 457(b) plans are rarely matched by employers.

Accumulation Stages—Accumulation stage refers to gaining assets during the early and middle years of employment: saving and investing for retirement.

Alpha—measures the difference between fund's actual return and its expected return based on the fund's beta and the actual returns of the comparable index. Alpha is often viewed as a measurement of the value added or subtracted by the fund's manager.

The problem reported by some professionals is that a positive alpha indicates that the fund performed better than its beta predicted and that the manager may or may not have anything to do with its growth. Perhaps the market itself contributed to the growth of the fund and the manager took credit when credit may not be supported by the data.

Annuities

Fixed annuity: a stream of unchanging payments for a specific period or for an individual's lifetime, depending on the terms of the annuity contract. They are sold by insurance companies to people who desire a fixed income.

Variable Annuity: An annuity with payments to the annuitant varies, depending upon the investment success of a separate investment account underlying the annuity. Because the invested funds are primarily in common stock, this annuity offers greater potential rewards and greater risks than annuities supported by fixed-income securities.

Immediate Annuity: An immediate annuity is a do-it-yourself private pension. When you retire, you give a lump sum of money to an insurance company, and it immediately starts paying you a monthly income for the rest of your life, no matter how long you live or what happens in the economy.

Equity Indexed Annuity: returns are based on the performance of an equity market index, such as the S&P 500, DJIA, the NASDAQ or other investments. The principal investment is protected from losses in the equity market, while gains add to the annuity's returns.

Tax Sheltered Annuities (TSA): commonly sold to public education institutions for decades. TSAs and 403(b)s are often interchangeable names for two very different retirement plans. TSAs don't provide additional tax deferment already allowed by the IRS for the 403(b).

Asset Allocation—Vital process of deciding how much of an investor's money to put into stocks, bonds, real estate, cash or other investments, based on age, goals, time horizon and the need, ability and tolerance to take risks.

Asset Classes—the core asset class of indexes and mutual funds are based on Market Capitalization, the relative size of the dollar value of the company: Large-cap, Mid-cap, small-cap, international, REITS. (See Lazy Portfolios).

The Barclay's Capital Aggregate Bond Index—a broad base index often used to represent investment grade bonds being traded in the United States. Index funds and exchange-traded funds (ETFs) are available to track this bond index.

Benchmark—group of stocks or bonds whose collective performance provides a standard against which to measure the returns of a mutual fund or other investment. Some widely used benchmarks are the Standard & Poor's 500 stock index, the Dow Jones Industrial Average, the Russell 2000 and the Wilshire 5000. The benchmarks used in this book to compare our portfolio are the NASDAQ composite, Barclay's Bond Index, and the European, Australia Far East (EAFE) Index.

Beta—measures the degree of change in value of a security that can be expected given a change in value in the comparable index or benchmark. A fund with a beta of one (1) indicates that the fund's value will move with the market. A fund with a beta greater than 1.0 is more volatile than its index and beta of less than 1.0 is less volatile than the index. A beta of 1.05 indicates it should perform 5% better than its corresponding index in an up market and conversely, 5% worse in a down market.

Blend/Core Funds—consists of a mix of growth and value stocks (see growth and value stocks definition).

Bogleheads Investment Philosophy—emphasize regular saving, broad diversification, and sticking to one's investment plan regardless of market conditions. The Bogleheads' approach begins with an investor deciding on percentage allocations to various asset classes, such as U.S. stocks, international stocks, U.S. bonds, etc. The desired allocations are then implemented using low-cost vehicles which are true to the targeted asset classes with taxes considered. Source: Bogleheads Wiki

Bogleheads—an idiom intended for ordinary investors to honor and follow Vanguard founder and investor advocate John Bogle's investing principles. The home of these investing enthusiasts is the Bogleheads Forum. The forum's regular posters discuss financial news and theory, while helping less experienced investors develop their portfolios, ALL FOR FREE! There are over 31,000 registered Bogleheads Forum users who normally make between 500 and 1,000 posts each day. Some members also participate in national or local chapter meetings. See reference section for information on two books written by Bogleheads authors. Source: Bogleheads Wiki

Book Value—The value at which an asset is carried on a balance sheet. It is the total value of the company's assets that shareholders would theoretically receive if a company were liquidated.

Bonds Maturity Dates—A type of fixed income security with a maturity, or date of principle repayment. They are classified as short-term, 1-3 years to maturity, intermediate 3-10 years and finally, long-term, 10 or more years. It is an important variable in the yield calculations. The intermediate-term bonds pay a higher yield than short-term bonds, but a lower yield compared to long-term (10+ years) bonds.

Broker—Individual who advises investors on stocks, bonds, mutual funds, or other investments and acts as an agent by buying or selling on the investor's behalf.

Broker/Dealer Firms—a person or a firm that trades securities for its own account or on behalf of its customers. Merrill Lynch and Morgan Stanley are well-know examples.

Capital Gain/Loss—Difference between an investment's original purchase price and the selling price.

Common Stock—Usually conveys voting rights and is often termed capital stock if it is the only class of stock that a firm has outstanding. Common stockholders are the residual owners of a corporation in that they have a claim to what remains after every other party has been paid. The value of their claim and the stock depends on the success of the corporation. Most stockholders own common stock as opposed to Preferred Stock.

Compounding—a mathematical function in which an investment's earnings also have additional earnings, leading to significant increases in value over time by accumulation of growth which includes the percentage of previous growth. Growth entails still more growth.

Corporate Earnings (or Earnings, Income)—Revenues minus costs of operating the corporation. AKA profits. Earnings are the reason corporations exist and are often the single most important determinant of stock prices.

Day Trader—a speculator who buys and sells stocks on the basis of small short-term price movements, often reacting quickly to good or bad news about a company or a sector, such as gold (See Speculation).

Defined Benefit Plan (Private and Public Pensions)—a retirement plan that pays employees a lifetime annuity when they retire. The employee does not manage or control the investments in this plan. In 1980, 38% of private sector workers were covered. Today, its 18% and falling.

Defined Contribution Plan—a retirement plan offered by employers that allows employees to contribute to the plan but does not guarantee a predetermined benefit at retirement (as opposed to a defined benefit plan): 401(k), 403(b) and 457(b).

Distribution stage—the time when an investor begins a plan for an orderly redemption of money for retirement living while protecting assets from major loses during a prolonged bear market.

Diversification—reducing stock market risk by investing in different types of stocks and bonds and different industries, or more simply, not putting "all of your eggs into one basket."

Dividend Growth—a share of a company's net profits distributed by the company to a class of its stockholders, usually on a quarterly or annual basis. The dividend is paid in a fixed amount for each share of stock held. This is one indicator that reflects the actual growth of stocks.

Dollar-cost averaging (DCA)—Investment of a fixed amount of money at regular monthly intervals or other schedule. This process results in the purchase of extra shares during market downturns and fewer shares during market upturns. DCA is based on the belief that the market or a particular stock will rise in price over long periods of time.

Emerging Markets—the stock markets of less developed countries. Countries usually included are Mexico, China, India, Thailand and Brazil.

Equities—another label for stocks, both common and preferred.

ERISA—Employee Retirement Income Security Act of 1974--the main law that sets standards for private pension plans, including the investment practices allowed in 401(k)s and in some 403(b)s and 457(b) employer sponsored plans.

Exchange-traded fund (ETF)—an index fund that trades on the open stock market as frequently as investors want. ETFs are purchased and sold through a broker (see Index funds.)

Expense Ratio—a mutual fund's annual costs, expressed as a percent of the fund's assets. This fee is disclosed in the fund prospectus.

Fee-only adviser—this financial advisor can only receive compensation directly from you. A fee-only advisor cannot receive compensation from a brokerage firm, a mutual fund company, an insurance company, or from any other source than you. When giving you advice only you and your interests are represented, see Fiduciary.

Fiduciary—individual entrusted with investment decisions on behalf of another. Is legally obligated to make decisions in the client's best interests. Currently, only independent Registered Investment Advisors (RIA) are required to act in a fiduciary capacity. Brokers or financial advisors working for a broker dealer firm or an insurance company are only held to a suitability standard (not a fiduciary standard). See Suitable Investments.

Financial Sales Pitch—attempts to alleviate or exploit the investors' natural fears of investing with a product, mostly insurance, that is frequently not in buyers' long-term interest.

Ginnie Mae Mutual Fund—A mutual fund that invests exclusively in government-backed mortgages and passes the interest payments to owners of the fund's shares.

Global fund—A mutual fund that invests in both United States and foreign securities.

Government National Mortgage Association (GNMA) —A government owned corporation that acquires, packages and resells mortgages and mortgage purchase commitments in the form of mortgage-backed securities.

Gross domestic product (GDP)—refers to the market value of all final goods and services produced within a country in a given period. It is often considered an indicator of a country's standard of living.

Growth Stocks—Companies whose earnings are expected to grow faster than average.

Hedge Fund—a fund that generally has the ability to invest in a wide variety of asset classes. These funds are often unregulated and use extremely risky leverage in an attempt to increase returns.

I Bond—A bond that provides both a fixed rate of return and inflation protected feature. The value of the bond increases with the total of the fixed rate and the inflation feature. The income is tax-deferred until funds are withdrawn (see treasurydirect.gov).

Index fund—Mutual fund that invests in all or a representative sample of the stocks that make up a benchmark, such as the S&P 500. The fund tries to match the returns of the benchmark.

Indexing Strategy—See Passive Management Strategy.

Individual Retirement Account (IRA)—a retirement account for people with earned income. Amounts contributed to traditional IRAs, Simple IRA, Simplified Employment Pension Plans (SEP), are usually tax-deferred and are held in the name of the purchaser. See ROTH IRAs.

Inflation—a rise in the general level of prices of goods and services in an economy over a period of time. When the general price level rises, each unit of currency buys fewer goods and services. Consequently, inflation also reflects erosion in the purchasing power of money – a loss of real value in our investments. A primary measure of price inflation is the annualized percentage change in the Consumer Price Index (CPI).

Initial Public Offering (IPO)—first public sale of stocks by a company.

Institutional fund—a mutual fund that is not available to individual investors, unless they meet a high initial investment. Typical clients are pension and profit-sharing plans and endowments.

Interest Rate Risk—the risk that interest rates will rise and reduce the market value of an investment. Long-term fixed-income securities, such as bonds, subject their owners to the greatest amount of interest rate risk. Shorter-term securities, such as treasury bills, are influenced much less by interest rate movements.

International Fund—a mutual fund that invests in non-U.S. securities.

Investment Policy Statement (IPS, informally known as a retirement plan or investment plan)—It provides the foundation for future investment decisions made by an individual investor or a formal oversight committee of an employer. It serves as a guidepost, identifies goals and creates a systematic review process. It keeps investors focused on their objectives during short-term swings in the market and provides a baseline from which to monitor investment performance of the overall portfolio.

Lazy Portfolio—comprised of low cost index funds that are broadly diversified in all of the major asset classes available: Large, mid, small cap, international, bonds, inflation protected and REITS. These portfolios are easy to monitor, rebalance and maintain. Also dubbed by their author/creator as either "dumb," "passive," "simple," "no brainer," "couch potato," "Coffeehouse," "2nd

Grader" and "cowards."

Life Cycle Funds (also called Target-date funds)—A special category of balanced, or asset-allocation, mutual fund in which the proportional asset class allocation in a fund's portfolio is automatically adjusted during the course of the fund's time horizon. This adjustment proceeds from a position of higher risk to one of lower risk as the investor ages and/or nears retirement. These funds are convenient, but investors need to determine if the asset allocation is right for their risk tolerance.

Liquidity—the ability for investors to get access to invested money quickly without redemption fees. Money Market accounts and bank savings accounts are well known examples. Fixed annuities are illiquid because of surrender fees, paperwork and other costs.

Loads—One-time fee charged to investors when they purchase mutual fund shares. Loads are usually assessed by brokers. A front-end load is paid up front and comes out of your initial investment: a back-end load, also called a deferred load and a redemption fee, is paid when you take your money out of the fund. Never pay a load to invest. NEVER!

Market Capitalization—Market Capitalization is based on the number of shares of stock outstanding (owned by investors) multiplied by the price per share of the company. The Market capitalization boundaries are

Mid Cap   = $2.5 – 10 billion
Large Cap = over $10 billion
Small Cap = Less than $2.5 billion

Modern Portfolio Theory (MPT)—the academic community found the following concepts: First, markets are too efficient (and fast) to allow traders or timers to exploit anomalies (sudden drops in value) in the prices of securities. Active management is therefore counterproductive trying to capture the opportunistic lower prices. Second, asset classes can be expected to achieve, over long periods of time, returns that are commensurate with their level of risk. Third, diversification across asset classes can increase returns and reduce risk. For any given level of risk, a portfolio can be constructed that will produce the highest expected return. Lastly, there is no perfect portfolio for everybody. Each investor must choose an asset allocation that reflects their ability, time horizon and risk tolerance.

Money Market Fund—Type of mutual fund that invests only in short-term instruments, not stocks or most types of bonds. Such instruments include commercial paper, bankers' acceptances and repurchase agreements. These funds are not insured by the Federal

Deposit Insurance Corporation (FDIC).

Mortgage-backed securities—bond type securities representing an interest in a pool of mortgages.

Municipal bond—the debt issue of a city, county, state or other political entity. Interest paid by most municipal bonds is exempt from federal income taxes and often from state and local taxes as well. The tax exemption stems from the use to which the funds from a bond issue have been devoted. The tax-exempt interest appeals to high net worth individuals.

Mutual Fund—an investment that allows thousands of investors to pool their money to purchase stocks, bonds or other types of investments, depending on the objectives of the fund. See Sector and Index funds

National Association of Securities Dealers (NASD)—an association of over-the-counter (OTC) brokers and dealers which establishes legal and ethical standards of conduct for its members. NASD was established in 1939 to regulate the over the counter (OTC) market in much the same manner as organized exchanges monitor the actions of their members.

Net asset value (NAV)—Market value of a mutual fund, minus its liabilities, expressed as a per-share figure. Mutual fund shares are sold or redeemed based on a daily NAV calculation.

New York Stock Exchange (NYSE°)—the trademarked name of the largest and oldest organized securities exchange in the United States. The NYSE, founded in 1792, currently trades about 85% of the nations listed securities. The Dow Jones Industrial Average's stocks are listed on the NYSE.

No-load fund—Mutual fund that does not charge any sales commission or other expense at the beginning or the end of the investment period.

Nominal Returns—Returns that have not been adjusted for the negative impact of inflation.

Panic selling—a flurry of selling in a particular security or many securities at once. Panic selling is accompanied by particularly heavy volume and sharp price declines as owners scramble to sell before prices drop even more. Panic selling is generally set off by an unexpected event viewed by traders as particularly negative. For example, uncertainty surrounding the outbreak of serious hostilities and a cutoff of oil supplies in the Middle East.

Passive Management Strategy—a buy and hold investment strategy, as opposed to an active management strategy. Typically, a passively managed portfolio purchases all securities that fit a desired asset class definition. The amount of each security

Steve Schullo and Dan Robertson

purchased is in proportion to its capitalization relative to the total capitalization of all securities in that asset class. Each stock is then held until it no longer fits the definition of that asset class.

Philosopher's Stone—The philosopher's stone was the central symbol of the mystical terminology of alchemy, symbolizing perfection at its finest, enlightenment and heavenly bliss.

Plan Document—a legal and required document by the Department of Labor (DOL) will describe the type of plan that an employer is offering, loan provisions, limitations of amounts deferred, distributions at employee termination of employment, rollovers to the plan and transfers, investment of contributions, plan termination, an employee's eligibility for participation, and rules for vesting.

Policy Wonks—they enjoy pontificating endlessly on subjects that most people are more than happy to know that someone else cares about. They have an annoying habit of throwing around arguments, statistics and examples that leave the uninitiated feeling, well...dumb.

Prospectus—a legal written document relating to a security offering that delineates the proposed business plan or the data relevant to an existing business plan. The information is needed by investors to make educated decisions whether to purchase the security. The prospectus includes financial data, a summary of the firm's business history, a list of its officers, a description of its operations and the mention of any pending litigation and expenses to the purchaser. A prospectus is an abridged version of the firm's registration statement filed with the SEC.

Qualifying Plan—An employer-sponsored tax-deferred employee benefit plan that meets the standards of the Internal Revenue Code of 1954 and that qualifies for favorable tax treatment. Contributions by an employee and employer matches accumulate without being taxed until distribution in an employee's retirement.

Real Estate Investment Trust (REIT)—a company that manages a group of real estate investments.

Rebalancing—the process of reinstating a portfolio to its original asset allocation. Rebalancing can be accomplished either through adding newly invested funds or by selling portions of the best performing asset classes and using the proceeds to purchase additional amounts of the underperforming asset classes.

Registered Investment Advisor (RIA)—A designation representing that a financial consultant is registered with the appropriate state regulators and has passed the required exams.

Return (also called Yield)-the percentage return on an investment.

A given investment can have a variety of yields because of the many methods used to measure yield.

Revenue Sharing—a compensation practice in which money is paid to the plan providers out of the annual expenses of investments. Revenue sharing is often hidden within the annual operating fund expense ratios. Thus, revenue sharing has been the principle reason for 401(k) lawsuits by participants who were not informed of these costs.

Risk tolerance (low)—an investor's unwillingness to accept one iota of short-term declines. Prefer to accept significantly less than average market returns in so-called "risk less" investments. Annuities, fixed accounts such as Stable Value and short term bonds in the accumulation stage are frequent products for low-risk tolerance investors. These are the folks that primarily fall prey to the annuity sales force. See Risk tolerance (high).

Risk tolerance (moderate)—the investors' ability and willingness to accept short-term declines in the value of equity (stock funds or indexes) investments without selling and without a worry in anticipation of greater gains to capture average market returns over the long-term. See Risk tolerance (Low).

Rollover—Reinvestment of a distribution from a qualified retirement plan into an IRA or another qualified plan in order to retain its tax-deferred status and avoid taxes and penalties for early withdrawal. Rollovers are used done upon retirement or changing employers.

Roth IRA—a tax-favored retirement plan. Contributions are not tax deductible. You pay taxes going into the Roth and that's all. Earnings are tax-free during accumulation and when withdrawn. Check for eligibility.

R-squared—reflects how closely the fund mirrors the comparable index and therefore reflects the percent of a fund's movement that can be explained by movements in its benchmark index. An index fund is usually 99% or 100% of the comparable index.

Rule of 72—A method of estimating the time it will take to double your money at a given interest rate:72 divided by the interest rate equals the number of years it will take for your money to double.

Russell 2000—the smallest 2000 of the largest 3000 stocks within the Russell index. Normally used as a benchmark for small-cap stocks.

Security—another word for stocks and bonds. See equities.

Sectors—Each sector carves out a narrow segment of the thousands of companies and their stocks. The idea is to put companies in similar industries together for comparison purposes.

The most common sectors in the S&P 500 Index are: basic materials, utilities, real estate, technology, healthcare, consumer goods, energy, manufacturing, finance.

Share classes—combinations of front-end loads, back-end loads and 12b-1 fees, by offering several different types of shares. Usually defined by a letter, share class A, B, C, D, E, and sometimes F. F is the best.

Sharpe Ratio—determines if the performance of a particular fund is worth the risk it assumes. Developed by Nobel Laureate William Sharpe.

Speculation—a financial action that takes above-average risks to achieve above-average returns usually during a short period of time. Speculation involves buying something on the basis of its potential selling price rather than on the basis of its actual value.

Spread—The difference between the price that the dealers pay to buy a stock or bond and the price at which they sell it. Also known as the "bid and ask" prices.

Standard and Poor's 500 Stock Index (S&P 500)—An inclusive index made up of 500 stock prices of the largest publicly traded corporations in the United States. The total capitalization of the index equals to about 80% value of the U.S. domestic stock market.

Standard and Poor's Midcap Index—an index designed to measure price movements of the stock of medium-sized companies. The index comprises the market value of all stocks of about 400 medium-sized companies.

Standard deviation—SD is a statistical measure of the volatility of a fund's short term return from the average long term return. The higher the SD, the greater the range of actual returns (higher or lower) compared to the average return, the greater the likelihood of risk.

Stock Market "Bubble"—takes place when market participants drive stock prices significantly above their value in relation to normal stock valuation (see stock valuation). The recent real estate and technology bubbles are clear examples.

Stock Options—Right to buy a defined number of shares in a company at a pre-set price, called the grant price, which is usually the market price on the day the option is awarded.

Style Drift—occurs when actively managed mutual funds go outside of their described style. For example, when a mid-cap fund holds a significant number of large-cap company stocks.

Stock Market (aka equity market)—the public entity of both physical and virtual space where shares (stocks) of public companies are traded on an agreed price (see Wall Street.)

Stock Valuation—the fundamental valuation is a measure which professionals use to justify stock prices. The most common example of this type of valuation methodology is P/E ratio, which stands for Price to Earnings Ratio. Historically the PE ratio for the S&P 500 has ranged between 7-11 but during recent bubbles, the ratio has risen to about 20 or higher.

Suitability Standard—usually means that brokers and advisers who work for commissions in broker/dealer firms need only suggest products that are suitable for your objectives, your income level and your age. No disclosure is required for possible conflicts of interest. See Fiduciary.

Taxable account—an account in which the securities are subject to annual federal, state and local taxes.

Third party administrator (TPA)—a company that processes employee benefit plans for a sponsoring employer for 401(k), 403(b) or 457(b) plans. This can be viewed as "outsourcing" the administration of the plan, since the TPA is performing tasks on behalf of the employer who is ultimately responsible for the plan. Employers normally pay for the expenses of the TPA for 401(k) plans. In 403(b) and 457(b) plans, the employee pays for most if not all of the employer's expenses of sponsoring the plan.

Timing the Market (Market timing)—Attempting to forecast market direction and investing based on the forecasts. Done by individuals who think they can beat the averages consistently.

TIPS (Treasury Inflation Protected Security)—similar to an I-Bond. A bond that receives a fixed rate of return, but also increases its principal by changes in the Consumer Price Index (CPI). Its fixed interest payment is calculated on the inflated principal, which is eventually repaid at maturity.

Treasuries—bonds the federal government issues to finance its debt, Treasury bills mature, or come due, in one year or less. Treasury notes can mature in from one to ten years and Treasury bonds have a maturity of ten years or more.

Turnover—the trading volume of the market or of a particular security or holdings within a fund.

Turnover rate—the trading volume in a particular stock or mutual fund during a time period, usually one year. For an investment company, the volume of shares traded as a percentage of the number of shares in the company's portfolio. A high turnover rate reflects frequent trading and may generate commissions for the manager. These trading costs are paid by the investor.

Value Stocks—stocks from companies that are selling for low prices relative to earnings and are out of favor with stock analysts.

See Growth stocks and Blend.

Value Tilt (advanced investors only)—Tilting is any change from a blend of both Growth and Value stocks to predominately Value stocks. Historical returns are greater with value stocks than growth stocks (Note: past returns are not predictive of future returns.)

Volatility—Amount of price fluctuation in the value of a stock, bond, mutual fund or benchmark. Measured by the Standard Deviation.

Wall Street—Reference to the entire investment community and a specific geographic area of Lower Manhattan where the NYSE, American Stock Exchange, and many of the largest investment banks and brokerage firms in the world and their employees, stockbrokers, analysts, traders, and financial news media are located.

Zero-Sum game—a situation in which one investor's gain must be matched by another investor's loss. Without considering taxes and transaction costs, many types of investing, such as options and futures, are examples of zero-sum games.

References

The inherent values in passive investment strategy are detailed in the works of Larry Swedroe, William Bernstein and Rick Ferri, and of course John Bogle. The most recent research cited and explained is found in Rick Ferri's latest book, *"The Power of Passive Investing."*

1. Bernstein, Peter, *Against the Gods: The Remarkable Story of Risk* John Wiley & Sons, Inc. 1996.

2. Bernstein, William, *Four Pillars of Investing* McGraw-Hill Inc., 2002.

3. Bernstein, William, *The Intelligent Asset Allocator* McGraw-Hill Inc., 2001.

4. Blodget, Henry *Facebook IPO Fiasco: Here's How Small Investors Got Rolled Over* Daily Ticker, May 24, 2012.

5. Bogle, John C. *Bogle on Mutual Funds* McGraw-Hill, Inc., 1994.

6. Bogle, John C., *Enough* John Wiley & Sons, Inc., 2009.

7. Bogle, John C., *The Clash of the Cultures: Investment Vs Speculation* John Wiley & Sons, Inc. Hoboken NJ, 2012.

8. Bogle, John C., *The Little Book of Common Sense Investing* John Wiley & Sons, NJ, 2007.

9. Borzi, Phyllis, *Challenges and Opportunities in Implementing the new DOL Participant Fee Disclosure Requirements,* General Session Presentation at the 2012 NAGDCA Annual Conference, San Diego CA.

10. Braham, Lewis, *The House That Bogle Built* McGraw-Hill 2011.

11. Brennan, Jack and the Vanguard Group, *Straight Talk on Investing: What You Need to Know* John Wiley & Sons, NJ, 2002.

12. Browne, Harry, *Fail-Safe Investing: Lifelong Financial Security in 30 Minutes* St. Martin's Press, 1999.

13. Buffett, Warren, quoted by Rana Foroohar, Time Magazine, January 23, 2012.

14. Chancellor, Edward, *Devil Take the Hindmost: A History of Financial Speculation* Penguin Group NY, 2000.

15. Covey Stephen R. *The 7 Habits of Highly Effective People* Free Press, 1989.

16. Denby, David, *American Sucker* Back Bay Books/Little Brown & Co. 2004.

17. Eisenberg, Lee, *The Number: A completely Different Way to Think About the Rest of Your Life* Free Press, 2006.

18. Esquith, Rafe, *There are No Short Cuts* Pantheon Books, NY. 2003.

19. Ferri, Richard, *All about Asset Allocation* McGraw-Hill, Inc. 2006.

20. Ferri, Richard, *All about Index Funds* McGraw-Hill Inc. 2007.

21. Ferri, Richard, *The Power of Passive Investing: More Wealth with Less Work* John Wiley & Sons, Inc. 2011.

22. Gladwell, Malcolm, *The Tipping Point: How Little Things Can Make a Big Difference* Little, Brown and Company, 2002.

23. Glason, George S. *Richest Man in Babylon* Penguin Group, 1955.

24. Grantham, Jeremy, quoted Chapter 3 in Lewis Braham, *The House That Bogle Built* McGraw-Hill 2011.

25. Hiltonsmith, Robert, The Retirement Savings Drain, Dēmos, Demos.org

26. Kinnel, Russel, *How a Fund's Expense Ratio Can Predict Its Success* Morningstar.com, April, 2007.

27. Kristof, Kathy, *Investing 101* Bloomberg, 2008.

28. Larimore, Taylor, Lindauer, Mel and LeBoeuf, Michael, *The Bogleheads' Guide to Investing* John Wiley & Sons, Inc. NJ, 2006.

29. Larimore, Taylor; Lindauer, Mel; Richard Ferri and Dogu, Laura F. *The Bogleheads' Guide to Retirement Planning* John Wiley & Sons, Inc. NJ, 2009.

30. Levitt, Arthur, *Take on the Street: What Wall Street and Corporate America Don't want you to Know* Pantheon Books, div of Random House, Inc. NY, 2002.

31. Lynch, Peter with John Rothchild, *Beating the Street* Simon & Schuster, 1993.

32. Mackay, Charles, *Extraordinary Popular Delusions and the Madness of Crowds* London: New Burlington Street, 1841.

33. Malkiel, Burton G. *A Random Walk Down Wall Street* W. W. Norton & Company, Inc. 2003.

34. Malkiel's, Burton G. and Ellis, Charles D. *The Elements of Investing* John Wiley & Sons, Inc. NJ, 2010.

35. Ney, Richard, *The Wall Street Jungle*, Grove Press, NY, 1970.

36. Norris, Floyd, *The Number of Those Working Past 65 Is at a Record High* New York Times, May 18, 2012.

37. Otter, Dan, *Teach and Retire Rich* Wise Guys, Inc. 2010.

38. Pond, Jonathan, featured in Dolores Kong's report in, *Don't Drive Yourself to the Poorhouse.* The Boston Globe, April 18, 2000.

39. Quirk, Daniel, quoted in Dolores Kong's report in, *Don't Drive Yourself to the Poorhouse* The Boston Globe, April 18, 2000.

40. Roth, Allan S., *How A Second Grader Beats Wall Street: Golden Rules Any Investor Can learn,* John Wiley & Sons, Inc. Hoboken, NJ, 2009.

41. Schultheis, Bill, *The New Coffeehouse Investor: How to Build Wealth, Ignore Wall Street, and Get on with Your Life* Penguin Group (USA) Inc. 2009.

42. Stanley, Thomas and Danko, William, *The Millionaire Next Door* Pocket Books, a division of Simon & Schuster, Inc. 1996.

43. Swedroe, Larry E. *The Only Guide to a Winning Bond Strategy You'll Ever Need* St. Martin's Press, NY 2005.

44. Swedroe, Larry E. *The Only Guide to a Winning Investment Strategy You'll Ever Need: Index Funds and Beyond* Truman Talley Books/Dutton, NY, 1998.

45. Swedroe, Larry E. *What Wall Street Doesn't Want You To Know: How You can Build Real Wealth Investing in Index Funds* St. Martin's Press, NY 2001.

46. Swedroe, Larry E. and Jared Kizer, *The Only Guide to Alternative Investments You'll Ever Need: The Good, the Flawed, the Bad, and the Ugly* Bloomberg Press, NY, 2008.

47. Swensen, David F., *Unconventional Success: A Fundamental Approach to Personal Investment* Free Press NY, 2005.

48. Thaler, Richard & Benartzi, Shlomo *Save More Tomorrow: Using Behavioral Economics to Increase Employee Saving* Journal of Political Economy, Vol 112 9(1) 2004.

49. Tobias, Andrew *The Only Investment Guide You'll Ever Need* Harcourt, Inc. 2002.

50. Toohey, Bill and Mary *The Average Family's Guide to Financial Freedom* John Wiley & Sons, 2000.

51. Vrana, Debora, *Estate of the Union* Money Makeover Feature, Los Angeles Times, December 10, 1996.

52. Wild, Russell, *Bond Investing for Dummies, 2nd Edition,* Wiley Publishing Co. NJ, 2012.

53. Wooden, John with Jamison, Steve, *My Personal Best: Life Lessons from an All-American Journey* McGraw-Hill, 2004.

54. Zweig, Jason *Your Money and Your Brain* Simon & Schuster NY, 2007.

Financial Websites

Bogleheads.org The best and most active investing website for the do-it-yourself investor found on the Internet. The Bogleheads, devotees of Vanguard founder and index-fund pioneer Jack Bogle, run a highly active online forum of more than 31,000 registered members. If you have time to sift through the posts (anyone can read and search the site without registering), the site offers a wealth of free investing advice—and it's not just for Vanguard investors. Under the forum's broad discussion topics, the Bogleheads chat about long-term indexing strategies, investing theory, ideas for building portfolios, and specific funds. You can also ask the group for help with your own portfolio (You'll have to register to write a post. It's free). Source: Bogleheads Wiki.

http://www.403(b)wise.com/ Founded by Dan Otter, PhD, Steve's warrior colleague to improve 403(b) plans. Packed with 403(b)/457(b) specific information, history, regulations, advocacy and a discussion forum. Dr. Otter is a teacher and financial trainer for classroom teachers who want to teach financial concepts to their students. Along with his wife Mandy, they created an educational product called the Portal. The Portal is a customized retirement plan website assisting Pre-K-12 school districts in providing financial education for their employees. It is available for LAUSD employees through their 457(b) plan. This is the second website that Steve follows and has written over 3,300 posts.

http://meridianwealth.wordpress.com/
Scott Dauenhauer's Blog. Writes articles on the problems with 403(b) investing and regulations. He is frequently cited and interviewed in the financial media. He is a consultant to CalSTRS and the co-creator (with CalSTRS excellent 403(b) team) behind CalSTRS Pension 2, a low-cost quality 403(b) plan available for California teachers.

http://www.nagdca.org/ The National Association of Government Defined Contribution Administrators, Inc is an outstanding professional organization. This website publishes articles, legislative debates and regulations pertaining to 403b, 401k and 457b plans. Their popular annual conference brings together benefits administrators for education and networking from all over the country. Unlike the history of the 403b where there was nobody to turn to, Steve found hundreds of like-minded professionals who want to do the right thing for the employees in terms of plan costs, fiduciary advice, transparency, accountability and oversight. All of these principles we detail in this book. The 403(b)Compare Web site is a bank of free objective information about 403(b) vendors and the products they offer.

http://www.dalbar.com/
Research institution that studies investor behavior.

http://www.morningstar.com Our portfolio is housed in the "portfolio" feature. Also has many investment forums, current articles, interviews and hundreds of research data and statistics.

http://www.yahoofinancial.com Great site to get information on investments via the ticker symbol.

http://www.vanguard.com
Where John Bogle started it all.

https://www.tiaa-cref.org/public/index.html
Provides low-cost 403(b) and 457(b) plan options.

http://www.treasurydirect.gov
Bond information: purchase Treasury bonds online.

http://www.ifa.com Indexing Fund Advisers. This site is packed with indexed/passive strategy information with data, research articles, charts, history, and interviews of well-known financial authors and academics. Indexing advisers are available for AUM fees.

http://www.fundadvice.com/home/ Another site for people who want the indexing investing philosophy with advisers available for an AUM fee.

http://www.dol.gov/ebsa/aboutebsa/main.html
The Department of Labor oversees Employee Retirement Income Security Act of 1974 (ERISA).

Research Your Employer's Plan

http://www.brightscope.com/ Rates 401(k)s. They are working on rating 403(b) plans at this writing.

The Following Financial Podcasts Support the Indexing Strategy and controlling spending.

http://paulmerriman.com/podcasts/
by Paul Merriman

http://itunes.apple.com/podcast/index-funds-advisors-podcast/id296274081 by Mark Hubner

http://itunes.apple.com/us/podcast/the-educated-investor/id317659246

https://personal.vanguard.com/us/insights/newsarchive/rss-audio-podcast-help

http://www.daveramsey.com/radio/home/?#podcast-tab Dave Ramsey talks about controlling debt, budgeting and reducing spending.

http://www.investmentadvisornow.com/investing-podcast.html by Larry Swedroe

Researching and Finding a Financial Adviser

Disclaimer About Financial Advisers: The authors have not used the services or any adviser from the four professional organizations listed below. We claim no guarantees about the ultimate cost schedules of any adviser found by any reader. The authors present them as a starting point, but the responsibility for finding a fee-only fiduciary who looks for your best interest is best assured only by the reader's preparation and is the reader's sole responsibility.

http://www.finra.org/index.htm FINRA is the largest independent regulator for all securities firms doing business in the United States. Choose the "Investor's" tab and learn how to protect yourself by finding out about your adviser or potential adviser.

http://www.dol.gov/ebsa/newsroom/ fsfiduciaryoutreachconsumers.html Department of Labor Guide Lines for finding a fiduciary adviser.

http://garrettplanning.com/
This professional organization has advisers available who charge by the hour "as needed" or by AUM. According to their website, no commissions or products that pay the adviser are recommended to clients.

http://www.napfa.org/ The National Association of Professional Financial Advisers organization has advisers who charge an AUM and/or by retainer, but not commissions or hidden fees.

Lazy Portfolio Websites from Chapter 9.

http://paulmerriman.com/ Paul Merriman's "Ultimate Buy and Hold" Portfolio

http://assetbuilder.com/ Scott Burn's "Couch Potato" Portfolio

http://www.rickferri.com/ Rick Ferri's "Four-Core" Portfolio

http://david-swensen.com/2008/10/27/
david-swensen-portfolio-for-small-investors/
David Swensen, Chief Investment Officer at Yale

http://www.daretobedull.com
Allan Roth's "2nd Grader" Portfolio

http://www.investorsolutions.com/ Frank Armstrong's "Ideal Index" Portfolio

http://harrybrowne.org/
PermanentPortfolioResults.htm
Harry Browne's "Permanent Portfolio"

http://www.investmentadvisornow.com/
Larry Swedroe's "Simple Portfolio"

http://www.efficientfrontier.com/ William Bernstein "No Brainer" Portfolio.

http://www.coffeehouseinvestor.com/
Bill Schultheis "Coffeehouse Investor" Portfolio

Additional Resource

http://www.403bcompare.com/ The 403bCompare Web site is a bank of free objective information about 403(b) vendors and the products they offer. This site was created to help employees of California's local school districts, community college districts or county offices of education make better-informed investment decisions. It is available for anyone seeking information about different retirement products that might be available in your employer sponsored plan or what you adviser might suggest.

Index

About the Authors

Stephen A. Schullo taught in the Los Angeles Unified School District (LAUSD) for 24 years and UCLA Extension. Steve wrote investment articles for union newspaper (circ. 50,000). Thrice featured retirement plan advocate in the Los Angeles Times and U.S. News and World Report. He started an investor self-help group for teacher colleagues and wrote 4,500 posts in three investment forums since 1997. Frequently quoted by the media, testified at legislative hearings, honored by the Los Angeles teachers' union for his retirement planning advocacy. He currently serves on LAUSD's Investment Advisory Committee and former co-chair. The committee monitors 457b/403b of 55,000 former and current LAUSD employees, worth $2.0 billion.

Dan Robertson Director of the Employment and Training Center for Persons with Disabilities at California State University, Los Angeles, taught Special Ed for twenty-eight years: elementary and graduate students. He managed job training programs by writing $3.5M worth of grants, created budgets and maintained financial oversight. With Steve, he was featured in the Los Angeles Times Money Makeover feature. Dan has twenty-five years of reflection, study and investing experience. Implemented a low-cost 403b plan at a GLBT recovery center. Dan and Steve are married and have been together for 37 years.

CPSIA information can be obtained at www.ICGtesting.com
Printed in the USA
BVOW03s0937301013

335030BV00011B/175/P